Jim Harries

**New Foundations for Appreciating Africa:
Beyond Religious and Secular Deceptions**

World of Theology Series

Published by the Theological Commission of the World Evangelical Alliance

Volume 9

Vol 1	Thomas K. Johnson: The First Step in Missions Training: How our Neighbors are Wrestling with God's General Revelation
Vol 2	Thomas K. Johnson: Christian Ethics in Secular Cultures
Vol 3	David Parker: Discerning the Obedience of Faith: A Short History of the World Evangelical Alliance Theological Commission
Vol 4	Thomas Schirrmacher (Ed.): William Carey: Theologian – Linguist – Social Reformer
Vol 5	Thomas Schirrmacher: Advocate of Love – Martin Bucer as Theologian and Pastor
Vol 6	Thomas Schirrmacher: Culture of Shame / Culture of Guilt
Vol 7	Thomas Schirrmacher: The Koran and the Bible
Vol 8	Thomas Schirrmacher (Ed.): The Humanisation of Slavery in the Old Testament
Vol 9	Jim Harries: New Foundations for Appreciating Africa: Beyond Religious and Secular Deceptions

Jim Harries

New Foundations
for Appreciating Africa:
Beyond Religious and Secular Deceptions

WIPF & STOCK · Eugene, Oregon

NEW FOUNDATIONS FOR APPRECIATING AFRICA
Beyond Religious and Secular Deceptions

Copyright © 2016 Verlag fur Kultur und Wissenschaft. All rights reserved. Except for brief quotations in critical publications or reviews, no part of this book may be reproduced in any manner without prior written permission from the publisher. Write: Permissions, Wipf and Stock Publishers, 199 W. 8th Ave., Suite 3, Eugene, OR 97401.

This edition published by Wipf and Stock Publishers in cooperation with Verlag für Kultur und Wissenschaft.

Wipf & Stock
An Imprint of Wipf and Stock Publishers
199 W. 8th Ave., Suite 3
Eugene, OR 97401

www.wipfandstock.com

PAPERBACK ISBN: 978-1-4982-9445-4
HARDCOVER ISBN: 978-1-4982-9446-1

Manufactured in the U.S.A.

Contents

Acknowledgements 7

List of Abbreviations..8

Glossary of Key Terms 9

Introduction and Summary..11

1. Searching for a Foundation in Africa...17

2. Women in Culture, Equality and "Bi-tegrity" 29

3. Language/Culture Conundrums that Lead to Misunderstandings.........37

4. New World Revealed and Its Implication.....................................41

5. The Problem of Foundationalism 47

6. Sin and Life..59

7. Finding a Foundation for Life 75

8. Undermining Has Been Undermined 87

9. Brave New World of One "Religion" 93

Bibliography..99

Biography 106

Acknowledgements

I am grateful for the editorial help I received from Prof. Thomas K. Johnson in the preparation of this text. Thanks especially to Marilyn James for doing the copyediting.

List of Abbreviations

AIDS   Acquired Immune Deficiency Syndrome

AVM   Alliance for Vulnerable Mission

BBC   British Broadcasting Corporation

BO   Body odor

NGO   Non-Governmental Organization

NIV   New International Version

Glossary of Key Terms

1) **Religion.** The understanding for religion that I use in this text is central to understanding of the text as a whole. The primary way I use religion is that it describes the life of people in almost any respect that is not secularism.

2) **The West/Westerners.** I consider "the West" to be those parts of the world predominantly populated by people whose culture has been profoundly influenced by developments in the western church for a period of one thousand years or more.

3) **Taboo.** "An interdiction that does not make rational sense" (from Priest, see below).

4) **Dualism.** The dualism that I refer to in this book, unless otherwise specified, is that which perceives and maintains a distinction between the spiritual and material or physical realms of life.

5) **Positivism.** "A philosophical system of Auguste Comte, recognising only positive facts and observable phenomenon, and rejecting metaphysics and theism" (Concise Oxford Dictionary, 1982).

6) **Secularism.** That which is not "religion."

7) **Bi-tegrity.** An expression of integrity arising from people forced to live under the authority of two systems that are mutually incompatible.

8) **Africa.** Africa, when referred to in this text, should be assumed to be sub-Saharan Africa. The author's understanding of African people arises primarily from where he has personal experience, in eastern and southern parts of the Continent. All African people are not the same. Some may not fit the descriptions that he gives.

9) **Foundationalism.** Asserts that there are essential beliefs that must be known and/or assumed before other truths can be known since those truths are built upon the essential beliefs. The essential beliefs are said to be self-evident, and are acquired through the senses and/or reason.[1]

---

[1] https://carm.org/dictionary-foundationalism

Introduction and Summary

Are there many religions, or is there one religion? The regular answer is that there are many. Yet the parameters of the term "religion" as used in the West are Christian. Perhaps the implicit default transfer of features of Christianity to other people's ways of life around the world that has been associated with the widespread use of the term religion is illegitimate, this book suggests. To be honest, in the historical development of the term "religion" and in the historical development of the West, there has only really been one well-known "religion." That is the Christian religion. Assuming that non-western people's ways of life are based in "religion" in the same way as is Christianity in the West has sometimes been to spread more confusion than light. It has made all other religions look like they are versions of Christianity.

The above is just one of many issues of contemporary life explored in this text. The author has lived amongst indigenous people in Africa from 1988 to date. In this text, he shares some of his experiences from the perspective of the development of his understanding of the nature of "religion." In this sense this book is very African. It builds, to an extent at least, on an African pre-suppositional base.

This book is about a pretentious obsession with secularism. Why refer to people's relationship with secularism as being a "pretentious obsession"? Secularism is in its origins clearly a branch, even if a heretical branch, of Christianity.[2] By turning a blind eye to this fact the academic and scholarly world constantly compromises the foundations of its research. Denying the Christian origins of secularism is misleading millions of people. It is trying to deny millions of people a true knowledge of God. Failing to impart a knowledge of God is indirectly causing massive suffering and death. Ironically, denying African people a true knowledge of God, this author suggests, is denying them comprehensive access to some of the benefits of the secularism currently being imposed onto them.

Science assumes the physical world is real and can be understood because the physical world stands under certain physical laws, the laws of

---

[2] "Christian secularism" was in mid-twentieth century a subject of hot discussion. Christian secularists argued in favor of a "relatively unreligious approach to life" as a historical outcome of Christianity to be freely embraced. Historically, the results of secularism have often been connected to the outcome, especially of liberal Protestant theology (Thomas K. Johnson, e-mail message to author, May 5, 2015).

nature. Science also assumes that people can learn to understand the physical world by means of disciplined observation, because our human sense abilities correspond with nature while good principles of reasoning correspond with the laws of nature. These assumptions largely arose from the biblical doctrine of creation, not primarily from secularism, whether or not western scientists were personally Christians. But after the influence of secularism in the West, these assumptions have assumed a life of their own, somewhat independent of their historical roots.

This text constitutes an appeal to the powers that be to please listen and to respond to the cry of the poor. Economic indices these days often show growth in African economies. They do not always show how dependent that growth is on charity. This charity is often deeply Christian in origin; but it is no longer interpreted in the light of the depth and breadth of Christian teaching. Such charity is resulting in dependency in the majority world, certainly Africa, of enormous proportions. Sometimes dependency is healthy and normal. Sometimes it is unhealthy. Many of the types of dependency that are these days booming are unhealthy. They are spelling doom and disaster for the days ahead. Urgent action is required. Things could be different.

African people are searching for a foundation for living. The natural world does not provide an adequate foundation for them. Hence Africa has long sought for a foundation in its beliefs in (so-called) witchcraft and spirit activity. As the natural world does not of itself provide an adequate foundation for human living, so the natural world does not contradict those beliefs. The secularism implicitly taught in educational systems throughout the African continent fails either to integrate with or to effectively challenge African traditional beliefs that perpetuate poverty. These beliefs being rooted in understandings of the divine are typically thrown out of court by secularism. The Christian roots of secularism that are often profusely ignored need to be engaged with perceived African and majority world realities. This is happening, but needs to be happening more. It is time for dominant western scholars to stop ignoring activity in the divine realm.

This text challenges the appropriateness of the transfer of certain supposed pillars of western society to Africa and the majority world. The adoption of global languages as languages of education and governance by African countries is shown to be causing endless problems. Material charitable aid is undermining local sensibilities. Human rights campaigns are, like secularism, a pseudo-Christian attempt at a solution to a problem. "Human rights" unfortunately fails to perceive many of the roots of the problems of our contemporary world. Anti-racist legislation in western nations renders majority world problems and important potential solutions invisible, this text suggests.

African and majority world ways of life make good sense according to their own ontological presuppositions. This is why communication oriented to bringing change needs to be impacting at the ontological level. If it is not, and African gods remain enthroned at the same time as western ideologies spread, African people are forced not into integrity, but into *bi-tegrity* (i.e., *dual-tegrity*). That is, they must please two masters; typically the West for its money, and their "gods" for life and security. Many of the perceived blights to development in Africa, corruption included, originate in this mandated *bi-tegrity*. I consider this issue in this text by looking at the plight of grandmothers, in the West and in Africa.

In order to not force people into bi-tegrity, I advocate, as I have in many of my writings: that some Westerners who seek to be of assistance to African people and their communities, should build at least some of their key relationships on local languages and resources. It is very difficult for Westerners ever to appreciate or even to discern the life-shaping role of African beliefs if they constantly bind themselves to positions of superior resource availability and language knowledge. When Westerners begin to use local languages and resources in service (what we call "vulnerable mission") they begin to see these things.

African people are not "blank slates" waiting to be written on by Westerners. That is why for Westerners to begin to grasp the impact of what they say and do in Africa requires a profound knowledge of what is already there. The new will not simply displace the old. The new will engage the old. Recognition of the "African world" is a pressing necessity. Secularism, because it easily regards traditional African beliefs as bunkum, is totally incapable of it. Secularism cannot engage what it perfunctorily disregards. Because European languages are these days deeply secular, such recognition requires the use of distinct languages (a different language in Africa as against in the West) and so an introduction of a process of translation to adjudicate communication between the West and Africa.

The absence of such a translation process puts long-term workers from the West in Africa into a pincer trap of misunderstanding, the sharpness of which is aggravated by their wealth (i.e., power) and use of outside languages. When there is no translation in communication between the West and Africa, then those who comprehend what is going on either must keep quiet, or be crushed by the pincer.

My experiences in my early years in Africa taught me that the solution to African problems can seem misleadingly straightforward to Westerners brainwashed by secular society to ignore African beliefs. The solution looks simple when one is only looking at half the problem. This becomes confusing, because formal education in most of Africa is an imitation of that in the West, so it advocates for western solutions. Secularism is misguided in its core assumptions. It supposes itself to be building "objectively" on "nature," while it is actually constructed on the back of Christian theology. Science and "objectivity" also are not rooted in science or objectivity, as was once thought. There is no scientific or objective foundation for them to be built on. Instead, they must be rooted in a "theology"—that deals with ultimate realities and their implications for life. Theology being omitted from globalized education systems, makes it very difficult for Africans to appropriate the benefits of secularism into their own communities.

Many in Africa believe that knowledge of European languages holds the key to health, wealth, and prosperity. Pragmatically for the short term it does. The use of European languages opens doors to access to outside resources. This access to outside resources then unfortunately adds to the problem(s) of dependency. Development thinking needs to be reconnected to Christian theology, so that the theology can engage with traditional beliefs. Such engagement needs to be mediated by African languages because only they can accurately encapsulate and communicate African people's beliefs. Only thus can development thinking sidestep the problem of using European languages that are a Trojan horse of western presuppositions. For sustainable development to occur requires the contents of the "Trojan horse" in western languages to be evident and visible. They are unfortunately rendered incomprehensible, and thus largely invisible in the process of translation into African worldviews.

The material or natural world does not provide a sufficient foundation of knowledge on how to live well. This has to come from beyond the natural world, i.e., from theology. The foundation for western development has come from Christianity. Thus the West's denying Christian theology to the majority world is like kicking away the ladder of development that they themselves used. For example, the means to enable African people to acquire a perception of a distinction between the material and the spiritual that can enable the development of science and the comprehension of "objectivity," are not to be found in the material world but in Christianity. Spiritual beliefs provide frameworks with which the observed world can be ordered. A case study on *sin* in this text shows how attacks on the Christian faith led by secularists, in this case particularly anthropologists, have been radically misguided: the western world in recent centuries re-defined sin in such a way that for it to be taken seriously it had to be "rational." That is, it had to make sense according to a western rational understanding. Later the notion that people had to live under "rational" sin was discredited. Some people did not realize that what was being discredited was what had anyway been misconceived. Discrediting it did not thus undermine Christian belief. Now superstructures built on non-foundations that seem to hang in the ether, have become hegemonic. These superstructures have enormous momentum in the West. Back peddling is necessary to undo damage caused by secular thought that otherwise, in so far as it undermines what is salvific (the Gospel of Christ and the foundation to life that it offers), can be considered homicidal.

The term religion as used in contemporary English has a strong implication that there is something in life that is *other-than-religion*. The dualisms[3] it sets up, of religious as against non-religious (i.e., secular) has been, once removed from its Christian roots, extremely deceptive. Such a feature of Christianity should not, this text suggests, simply be blindly presupposed to similarly exist in other ways of life (i.e., "religions") around the world.

Failure to recognize the foundational ontologically determinative role of Christian belief in the history of the West results in a ridiculous position in which science seems to be rooted in "chance." Urgent correction to this anomalous understanding is needed for the sake of a prosperous peaceful future for the contemporary fast globalizing world. Correction will come, according to this text, through champions ready to buck the system by living radical lives of discipleship and commitment to Christ in intercultural context. Only thus by demonstrating Christ-alive to contemporary times can the structures of secular deception be revealed for what they are and overturned in favor of eternal truths. The enormous apparent success of secularism globally reflects its Christian underpinnings. Yet as it is, as a supposed opposite to the "religion" on which it was built, its claims are misleading. Basic wrongs need righting, and misleading categorizations must be undermined by the above champions for the world to be a better place tomorrow.

The reader of this text should realize the plasticity of some of the terms used in it. This kind of plasticity, while normal to language use, is particularly prominent in this text because:

---

[3] Details of the dualisms concerned vary, as do the understandings of secularism that people work with. (Calhoun et al., *Rethinking Secularism*, 9 and 20.)

1) As a result of my writing while living and working in East Africa and functioning very much within the indigenous community, I am inclined, consciously or otherwise, to use terms in East African ways.
2) The nature of this text is such as to undermine the secular foundation on which the very English used to write it is based.

Many of the insights underlying this work have been acquired using phenomenological research methodologies. Beyond this paragraph, no further justification for such a methodology is given. Phenomenology is here considered justified, and in fact any denial of the use of phenomenology I think should be questioned, on the basis that phenomenology is foundational to normal human epistemology, i.e., learning. To use phenomenological method in research is then, effectively, simply to learn as people normally learn. Sometimes use of phenomenological method can result in expressions that appear to be ungrounded generalizations. The reader should bear in mind that when cultures differ, as between European and many African people, some differences will be generic in nature. What may appear to be ungrounded generalizations in this text, may actually be negations of incorrect generalizations otherwise held by default in western society. The phenomenological method used here is Christian, i.e., it recognizes the activity of spiritual forces in a way that secularists might not.

While rooted amongst other things in the author's experiences of Africa, this text does not specifically seek to address African people. The pre-suppositional base that is drawn on is not "African." The European language being used is correctly understood on the basis of numerous presuppositions that are often absent or unknown to many African people. I believe that other texts ought to be written to address African people in a way that can make sense to where they are coming from. Admittedly this is difficult to do, if only because much literacy in Africa is in European languages. That is a problem that this text attempts to address. African people can seem to be constantly bombarded with what is foreign and "better." I do not seek to add to such bombardment. African and other non-western people are of course welcome to read this text, but are asked to bear the above in mind.

1. Searching for a Foundation in Africa

Elijah Oloo was crowned King of Africa in Western Kenya in 1933.[4] Around seventy years later I attended a ceremony at which a flag was raised in memory of that momentous event. I stayed in the home of the grandson of the late "King." Yet, that particular "kingdom" is not remembered for having been particularly consequential on the world scene. Few know about King Elijah Oloo. Alfayo Odongo Mango, one of those involved in crowning him as king, has managed to achieve longer-lasting fame. He is said to have prophesied an end to colonial rule. It must have been hard in the 1930s to have imagined an East Africa free from colonial rule. Yet thirty years later in much of Africa, including Kenya, colonial rule did indeed come to an end.[5]

Alfayo Odongo Mango's father had been killed by mercenary soldiers in 1896 in an attack backed by the British. As a result of his death, Mango's mother took her young son to refuge at her own home in Ulumbi in Gem.[6] It was in Ulumbi that Mango first came across Christianity.[7] He was later converted as a result of being healed from serious illness involving convulsions and epilepsy.[8] Mango was in due course ordained as a deacon in the Anglican Church. Then in 1932 he left the Anglican Church and founded[9] the church of *Jo-Roho*.[10] (*Jo-Roho* could be translated into English as "people of Spirit." *Roho* is widely used to translate the English term Spirit. Hence the term *Roho* can be used for other churches that are not *Roho* churches as such, but are spiritual in their orientation.) Two years later in 1934 Mango was killed in an outbreak of violence aimed at this

---

[4] Anderson, *African Reformation*, 154.
[5] Ibid.
[6] Ogot, *Reverend Alfayo*, 109. I have personally lived in Ulumbi, the same village in which Mango's mother was born, for a number of years, and continue to have close relationships with that village.
[7] Ibid., 111.
[8] Ibid.
[9] Although Ogot depicts Mango as "founder" of this church, he also indicates that it had "its origins in the activities of Lawi Obonyo, a carpenter, and Syvano Nyamogo Odongo" (Ibid., 120) suggesting that while Mango might have formalized what was going on he was not actually its initiator.
[10] Ibid., 120. It should be noted that we are here discussing the founding of the *Jo-Roho* movement amongst the Kenya Luo tribe. The term *Roho* is widely used to describe many other movements and churches beyond the boundaries of the Luo tribe, whose founding arises from different if related histories.

new church. "It is reckoned that ten people, including Mango, were burned to death and about forty injured. Alfayo Odongo Mango seems to have sat in his house reading the Bible awaiting death at a time when all of his followers escaped," Ogot recounts.[11]

W. E. Owen, archdeacon of the Anglican Church in Kenya at that time, described his encounter with *Jo-Roho* religion by saying: "Well, it has been one of the weirdest experiences of my life, and it gives rise to much thought."[12] This is what, according to Hoehler-Fatton, caused Owen to exclaim in that way:[13]

> *Roho* churches cultivate an atmosphere in which people can let go and experience spiritual power in a variety of ways. Some believers speak in tongues, some jump up and down, some collapse in a trance. Women known as *laktache* (healers or doctors) are ready to restrain ecstatic dancers who are out of control. They also guard unconscious individuals whose souls are believed to have temporarily left their bodies. The archdeacon witnessed two participants in a deep trance, each tended by a woman, but just as he could make no sense of the 'hysterical' dances before him, neither could he comprehend this situation.[14]

Hoehler-Fatton is at pains to point out that the *Jo-Roho* (from hereon I will simply refer to it as *Roho*) movement is not foundationally a break away from the Anglican Church. She traces its roots much earlier: "In short, oral evidence places Mango and Lawi [Obonyo][15] in a continuum of charismatic grassroots Holy Spirit religion, well established by the time the missionaries constituted any real presence in the region."[16]

Owen experienced the above in 1933. A lot has happened since then. My first encounter with the *Roho* movement was in 1993, sixty years on. While a lot has changed, the movement continues. Now in 2015, I find myself having close relationships, stretching back over twenty-one years, with many ongoing branches of the same movement. I do suspect that Hoehler-Fatton is correct, and that the movement did not start with Anglicans in Western Kenya. Rather, before the Anglicans came along, there was already a movement. That very indigenous movement, with apparent

---

[11] Ibid., 125.
[12] Hoehler-Fatton, *Women of Fire*, 10.
[13] Ibid., 9.
[14] See http://www.youtube.com/watch?v=X8U90nX1l58 and http://www.youtube.com/watch?v=v07nh_vhPHc for you tube videos of contemporary churches that have emerged from the original *Jo-Roho*.
[15] Lawi Obonyo was a colleague of Mango's in the new *Roho* sect.
[16] Hoehler-Fatton, *Founders and Foundresses*, 396.

1. Searching for a Foundation in Africa

links to activity in late nineteenth century Uganda,[17] has variously engaged with Christianity and with the Christian church, including Anglicanism. The context in which an indigenous-founded movement engages profoundly with Christian belief, is to me a fascinating one. Unlike so much of "mission-Christianity," this is a movement that is foundationally deeply African. There is typically no dependence on western money or western languages in *Roho* churches.

People's traditions can be almost constantly in view in the practice of *Roho* church life. The extent to which this is the case may even not be noticed by someone unfamiliar with the Luo language or the depth and breadth of the taboos that Luo people live by.[18] Breaking taboos (or laws, the term commonly used in *Dholuo* is *chike*) sets up particular dynamics in the spiritual realm. Such dynamics are the focus of attention in *Roho* worship. *Roho* leaders, healers, and prophets are there to assist people who are facing untoward spiritual circumstances. Backing the efficacy of taboos are ancestral spirits. Engagement with *Roho* is a means of challenging, persuading, dissuading, circumventing and bringing about what is considered a helpful counter to untoward ancestral forces. Many people live in fear regarding taboos that they might have broken, knowingly or inadvertently. Others are concerned that jealousy and other forces are resulting in their being bewitched. The power of witchcraft is also connected to ancestral forces.

Roho churches build on the African context in which their members find themselves. This gives them particularly strong indigenous roots. Their members have no doubts about the reality of witchcraft and spirits. Witchcraft and spirits constitute the part of the spiritual foundation on which *Roho* churches ground their practices. They certainly do not shrink from overt action oriented to countering the activities of untoward spirits or witches. They like to hear from people who have been "possessed." Arguably such possession may be by the Holy Spirit, or by angels, but it seems very evident that ancestral spirits are often given credit. People so possessed may, amongst other things, have insights that can help them to identify witches. *Roho* churches are succeeding in providing a foundation for life that is distinct from the practice of witchdoctors and traditional healers, and that engages with Christianity in profound ways. The above

---

[17] Hoehler-Fatton, *Women of Fire*, 206.
[18] For an example that illustrates the complexity of the traditional Kenya-Luo legal code, see Raringo, *Chike Jaduong*, a pocket book listing 331 taboos to be followed to bring prosperity and avoid death.

are some of the reasons why some Christian missionaries and other churches in Kenya want to give *Roho* churches a wide margin.[19]

There has been a long tradition of planting churches in Africa using foreign languages and foreign material and financial support. This has been in many ways an incredibly successful strategy. In other ways, it has brought many problems in its wake. One of those widely recognized problems is that of the prosperity gospel. Another is unhealthy dependency, often financial, of the African church on the West. I wonder if there might not be room for discovering some new missiological insights through consideration of how functioning *Roho* churches have got to be where they are: how can they function and thrive without outside support?

Of particular interest to me in this text are the foundations that *Roho* believers lay. As I will discuss further below, the modern West has in recent centuries endeavored to interpret their foundations for living as if they have been laid in secularism. That is, the West has believed that science is built on objective foundations and that life should be founded on the same basis. Since the 1950s, the West has had to realize that there are no absolute foundations on which science can be laid. Instead, science has been laid on foundations built in a context of much influence by Christianity. That is to say, it was the historical development of the western world, under the influence amongst other things of Christianity, that enabled the development of science. While the belief that science is somehow foundational continues on the basis of prior momentum, the secular project has as a result of the above realization acquired a major flaw. As a result of this I would like to ask: if there is no objective foundation on which science and modernism can be built, then how are the benefits of these things to be passed on to people who are living outside of the secular West, particularly in view in this text, to Africans? If the West acquired science by building on Christianity as foundation, is this a necessary route also for Africa to follow? That is in other words; is the project of encouraging development in Africa best achieved by encouraging the Christian faith?

---

[19] There has been a long debate on whether indigenous Christian movements in Africa, such as the *Roho* church described above, are bringing people to Christ or taking them away from Christ into their traditions. For more on this debate, see Sundkler, *Bantu Prophets*. My own position is to say that we need to reach out to people in these churches, and that they can help us to understand African Christianity that needn't be oriented to dependency or the modern prosperity gospel.

1. Searching for a Foundation in Africa

In this text I explore the means by which *Roho* believers in Africa search for and build a foundation for their lives, and especially ways in which they draw on Christianity to do so. My experience working with *Roho* believers is that they are pragmatic and eclectic in what they build and how they build. We could say that *Roho* believers draw on all available sources of understanding. In other words, unlike what underlies many efforts by Westerners at isolating "truth," they do not distinguish between things that are "real" and things that are "not real." Those two categories do not seem for them to exist.[20] A very apt question for modern man who is concerned about the rest of the world to ask himself is: now that the once-held belief that there is some objective basis in ultimate objective truth on which to build one's life has been undermined,[21] how does one build a foundation for life?

I would like to suggest that the *Roho* view of Christianity is one of excitement. That is—*Roho* believers, whose predecessors at one time functioned as parts of non-Christian movements, are excited to have discovered Christianity. Unlike the situation of their forefathers, who had no authoritative texts to draw on, *Roho* believers have access to the Christian Scriptures. The Luo people of Kenya, for whom Christian Scriptures are already translated into their own language and are widely available, have access to something that their forefathers were not aware of. *Roho* believers, then, who are eclectically drawing on diverse sources for their life's foundation, are at the same time excited to find something new in Christ. The Bible has great prominence for them. Many of their leaders and their laity draw heavily on it for guidance. The nature of the message of the Bible is in many ways quite unlike that of their traditions. Luo traditions are rooted in a multiplicity of spirits of diverse ancestors, frequently seeming to contradict one another and with no apparent teleological purpose beyond maintaining the cycle of life, from birth to death and around again. The Bible, however, talks of an ultimate creator God who has an apparent plan for human existence that includes a beginning and an end. The Bible is leading *Roho* believers towards an understanding that there is a unified meaning and direction to life. The foundation for meaning and direction that they are discovering is not scientific objectivity. It is the Gospel of Jesus Christ.

Roho people's engagement with the Bible and their experience and perception of Christian churches around them is empowering. I suggest also that it is not sufficient. They should not be expected to be able to be-

---

[20] See more discussion on this below.
[21] See more on this below.

come "fully-fledged Christian churches," that is, without a deepening of their relationship with older churches around the world including in the West. A deepening of such relationship is however made difficult by a number of factors. One of these is that African branches of historical churches (in which category I here include mission churches like Anglican or Catholic, but also Pentecostal and other "newer" churches) that they ought to be drawing from, have not themselves developed indigenous foundation(s). Instead, it seems almost universally that churches in Western Kenya draw their authority from sources in other parts of the world, typically the West. Those sources that claim to be authoritative if not hegemonic, are in English. The same English has been and continues to be profoundly influenced by now defunct notions of foundationalism, mentioned above.[22] This kind of implicit content to English can make it very difficult if not impossible for African people to appropriate theology from the West at any depth into their own lives and worldviews. Although there are certainly differences between *Roho* and other churches in this part of the world, the differences are on a sliding scale. People in other-than-*Roho* churches are also African, and so essentially have the same historical background as do *Roho* believers. Thus they have many of the same difficulties in appropriating western theology. They are also faced with the need to try to appropriate theology that is rooted in different cultural contexts, including a presupposition of "classical foundationalism" that is both incorrect, and that local Kenyan Christians do not share. They tend to be more intent, for various often good reasons from their point of view, at imitation of western churches and church practices than at trying to understand things themselves.[23] Western mission-founded churches in Africa frequently conceal the degree to which they are guided by African traditions that *Roho* churches express openly.

African people who are "emerging from animism" will inevitably take a different approach to the Scriptures and to faith in Christ than the approach that is and has been taken by historical Christian churches in western nations. The truth of this is often not recognized by people in the West. If it is recognized, African people are encouraged to "let go of" their traditions. Their traditions after all are untoward, if not evil.[24] As a

---

[22] Classic foundationalism that, according to Plantinga, is defunct (Plantinga, *Reason and Belief*, 62).

[23] Basic amongst these "good reasons" is the need for ongoing funding from western Christian bodies, which requires at least apparent compliance with practices coming out of notions of foundationalism rooted in reason that African Christians struggle to understand and certainly do not share.

[24] Douglas, *Sorcery Accusations*, 178.

1. Searching for a Foundation in Africa

result, presumably of this kind of pressure, many Kenyan people will in my experience say that they have "left their traditions." For Kenyan people, not to claim to have "left one's traditions" is in today's world asking for mockery if not ridicule. Even worse than mockery and ridicule, in a sense, is the risk that such would put African people in a very difficult position regarding their relationship with the West. An increasing number of western-led organizations and initiatives are ever thicker on the ground in Africa.[25] These organizations are providing a larger and larger piece of the cake that local people are eating. There is a reason these organizations come from the West (i.e., the part of the world deeply influenced by the western church). They are trying to bring "correction" to things happening on the ground in Africa. They perceive the African situation as lacking. Thus they have two broad alternatives. Their preferred alternative is to see the context as unfriendly but the people as sound. On the basis of this presupposition, African people can be funded to enable them to change their own communities and physical contexts. The other alternative is to see the African people themselves as part of "the problem."[26] Following this alternative, if African people are perceived by the West as continuing to be "part of the problem" that is preventing Africa from being what it should, then how can the same African people be used to bring about the changes? If they cannot be so used, then the jobs of millions of them who are depending on foreign charity in their employment in diverse internationally rooted organizations are at risk.[27]

Good intentions are highly valued in western nations. That such an approach of valuing good intentions should be dominant is not surprising. Good intentions are important, and knowing how things work out sufficiently well to justify all one's actions on the basis of long-term results is complicated after all! Yet surely it must be important to ask how the actual helpfulness of the said good intentions is to be assessed. Surely there must be some effort at measuring the outcome of the "good intentions"? If there is no means of assessing the outcome of actions arising from good intentions, then we have no way of knowing whether the said "good intentions" are actually proving to be helpful at all, especially in the long term.

---

[25] Bronkema, *Flying Blind?*
[26] An acknowledgement of people as being a part of "the problem" ties in closely with Christian notions of sin. In order to overcome sin people need, according to Christian belief, to be re-born (John 3:3) and to experience a renewing of their minds (Rom 12:2).
[27] So are, of course, the jobs of the people who are living off what the above people are spending, or who are dependent on them in various endless ways.

The question of good intentions addressed above is, it seems to me, implicitly linked to that of biblical interpretation. A lot of people's actions are deontologically rather that teleologically motivated. Deontology is about duty. The utmost end of Christian deontology is God. That is, Christians faithfully do their duty knowing that God has ordained them to do so. Hence they do not necessarily do what they do because they themselves comprehend all its beneficial outcomes. Instead, they function deontologically according to an interpretation of God's commands. They trust, if you like, that God knows what he is doing, and so that if they follow his commands they are on the right course. Wrong or non-understanding of God's commands puts one at risk of practicing deontology that is disconnected from the ultimate teleology (i.e., God). This is a serious phenomenon troubling contemporary society. Contemporary society in the West ceased to be overtly guided by God some centuries ago. This means that instead of *refreshing* their understanding of God, secularists are functioning on the basis of once-believed-theologies that may now be outdated. That is—instead of doing needful theology themselves, secularists in the West are simply assuming that the theological pre-suppositions put in place at the time of the founding of secularism are eternal. Questioning of those pre-suppositional foundations would require a renewed attention to prayer, to the Scriptures, to the tradition of the church, to prophecy, and to inspiration from God himself; things that secularists are loath to get involved in. Since the undermining of foundationalism, however, if secularists are not building on an objective foundation because there is none, then they must be building on a theological foundation. If secularism were to be building on a totally secure theological foundation then presumably it would be legitimate to add to it layer after layer of new understanding. If however, as we have discovered above, secularism is building on what may now be in part an outdated theological foundation, then it risks continuing to build on that which despite good intentions will not bring good outcomes. Frankly, theology has never been something that is "done once" and then ignored forever after. Every generation has had to have its own theologians. Ignoring this requirement seems to have put secularism onto a very shaky foundation. It should be little wonder then that (in its western formulation) it often makes little sense to African people.[28]

Some African people have been keen to adopt what they perceive to be western ways. Often they have had no choice but to do so. Some who

---

[28] In practice, African people develop their own understandings of "secularism," as discussed further below.

have not been quick to imitate the West have been left pauperized, and are considered backwards in their own communities. Unfortunately however, many have not had a deep grasp of the nature of the foundations coming from the West that they have been imitating. This should of course not be surprising to us, as neither have the Westerners who have been living those foundations (as discussed above).

People are born into communities that function in certain ways. A new generation typically accepts most of the presuppositions of their forefathers as legitimate. (If they do want to change some presuppositions, then they do so in the context of the broader set of presuppositions that they have inherited.) What was once a historical impact has for a subsequent generation become a "norm." Within a particular community, such a "norm" can easily be considered to be a universal human norm. Studies by anthropologists amongst others have revealed that many norms that might colloquially be considered universal are actually very peculiar. That is, there is great diversity in the traditions (i.e., "norms") of different people around the world. Some African people have been quick to take on board many of the visible and easily "learnable" aspects of western ways of life (for example the things that constitute school curriculum). They have not necessarily been able to appropriate underlying presuppositions from the West. These presuppositions, sometimes considered by many Westerners to be "universal norms," are actually not universal at all. (Many of the norms that the West holds as "universal" arise, I suggest, from its peculiar Christian history.) Hence use of western languages and western curricula in education in Africa all too often forces students to break with the fundamental educational principle which says that learning should go from known to unknown. Instead students go from unknown to unknown. This can very seriously interfere with the acquisition of understanding in ways which in practice lead to ongoing unhealthy dependence of Africa on the West.

The use of western languages in Africa has become very "normal." Some argue that some western languages, such as English, have become African languages. That may to some extent be the case. Unfortunately that being the case does not of itself resolve the potential problems that use of English in Africa by African people brings. Those countries or communities that have adopted European languages "as their own" are nowadays often under an intense pressure, that no one could have predicted a few decades ago, to conform to western ways of using what they thought was their language. This pressure emerges from so-called globalization. As a result of globalization, native English speakers' activities penetrate more and more what were previously obscure corners of the globe, often not through their physical presence but through their technological reach, for example, through the internet. This pressure to conform to a foreign standard, usually backed by funding that is dependent on the same, makes it more and more difficult for people to use the language concerned in sensible ways for their own purposes. Thus use of a European language can have the effect of rendering people less and less competent in the running of their own communities' affairs.

I hope my reader is clear that the reasons that I give in favor of the use of indigenous languages are not so as to preserve museum pieces.[29] Use of indigenous languages enables people to speak sensibly about their own contexts, including the traditions and cultures that are a part of them that they have inherited from previous generations.

I have looked at some of the problems of the provision of material aid in more detail in my 2011 paper.[30] I have mentioned above that it is material dependency on outside aid that is forcing majority world people, certainly many in Africa, into incompetency in managing their own affairs. One reason for this is because providers of aid require things to be done, or at least communicated back to them, in ways that make sense to them according to their pre-suppositional base and understanding, not the understanding of the people being "helped." Because aid comes hand in hand with a certain language, typically a European language, dependency on aid strongly encourages use of the same European language. In other words—because those with a good knowledge of European languages are the ones who get primary access to aid, this provides an incentive to the thorough learning of European languages that do not actually aid in acquiring effective self-understanding.

I have looked at the question of human rights in more detail elsewhere.[31] There have been many critics of the human rights approach to life, including for example Mutua.[32] Human rights tends to be very individualistic. It looks at the rights of individuals rather than their social obligations to others. For example, human rights will not emphasize the "obligation" of a mother to rear her child or the right of a child to a mother. My main critique of human rights is probably that it is too abbreviated a version of the full text of Scripture. Being very brief, it fails to

---

[29] I do not decry those who want to preserve languages for their own sake. I am sure there are many good reasons for doing so. Yet, that is not my point in this book.
[30] Harries, *Immorality of Aid*.
[31] Harries, *International Development*.
[32] Mutua, *Human Rights*.

1. Searching for a Foundation in Africa

provide anything like the profundity of guidance that the whole Bible can provide.[33] The declaration of human rights is much too simplified a "creed" on which basis to evaluate contemporary events without reference to the wider body of Scripture.

It is not often enough mentioned in Africa that the principles behind protecting human rights are partly biblical in origin, principles such as recognizing that our neighbors are created in God's image and God wants us to love our neighbors. Similar to the way the assumptions about nature and science which arose from the Bible have been separated from their biblical roots, so also public discussion of "human rights" has often been separated from the Godly roots of the principles. And once this happens, people, especially in the West, have used the language of human rights to say things that sound absurd in Africa.

Anti-racist policies as practiced in western nations should also be mentioned at this point. These policies are probably set up with good intentions in mind. They intend to protect non-native western people in western nations from "unfair" bias. At the same time the same policies result in serious problems. I have articulated these in more detail in another article.[34] Racial policies designed for use within the West can in today's globalized world quickly come to have a much wider reach. This means that norms that western countries set up as standards for western homelands become global norms. This is a great irony, but it seems rarely to be noticed. So in much of North America, for example, it is "illegal" to treat someone of African origin differently than one would treat someone of European origin. (The standard taken is usually the western-born white person.) When this same standard becomes globalized, it means that an African person living in Africa still has to be treated as if they are a white person from Europe. This effectively renders people into being strangers in their own homes.

North Americans are raised to believe emphatically that they should not treat people differently according to their color. They cannot simply "drop" this orientation when they get to Africa. Instead what they must do is to treat all Africans as if they are North Americans. They may well continue to do this for a long time in the face of enormous amassing evidence to the contrary, so deeply ingrained has the message of "not being racist" been drummed into them. What has been drummed into them

---

[33] In stating this I am pointing to the fact that the declaration of human rights is a type of contemporary creed drawn up on a biblical foundation, but using in part secular reasoning.
[34] Harries, *Anti-Racist Strategies*.

throughout their life in the West is that everyone regardless of their color and origins should be treated the same as Westerners. This means zero taking into account of cultural background and different ways of using language. Should an American come to the position in which he will treat African people differently to the way that he treats his fellow Westerners back home, he had better look out. He may bump into a queue of people looking to condemn him for being a grossly biased racist, in addition to another queue of people who have already condemned him for behaving paternalistically while in Africa.

Books, educational courses, the television, the internet, radio, advertisements, clothing, sexual fashions, and many other things all coming predominantly from the West, enforce the same presuppositions onto non-western people: "appear to be the same as us, or be wrong!" The issue of the recent acceptability of homosexual relationship comes to mind here. When they were being ostracized in the West, as they were for hundreds if not thousands of years, of course Africa was expected to follow suit. Now that a few years ago it was decided that such ostracism should stop, threats are made to withdraw funding from those in Africa who might deign not to comply.

In concluding this section, we can say that the strong message coming from the West backed by western languages and resources is: do not have any foundation other than the one we are giving you. In effect the West says "we are the provider of the foundation that you need." *Roho* churches are considered syncretistic. Use of African languages is considered primitive. Trying to rescue one's own languages is considered a waste of time. Wearing other than western clothes may be quaint, but is not likely to be considered practical. Belief in God is considered foolhardy. Education in other than English is sub-standard. Every latest fad from the West must be welcomed with open arms and responded to instantaneously without exception, even if the West itself has only recently come to a different decision on something. Africa is looking for a foundation. Developing Africa could be encouraged to build a foundation on Christianity. The West is determined though, it seems, to give them only caustic secularism.

2. Women in Culture, Equality and "Bi-tegrity"

These days, it seems, international and intercultural relationships are much about money. The baseline for justice itself is often money. Some in our global community are doing their utmost to try to bring about international economic equality.

There is a lady known to me, who was widowed long ago, whose small dirty one-roomed house almost caved in on her. The fire for cooking was in one corner of her house. The bed was alongside another wall. The other wall had a few tatty chairs backed up to it. Between chairs and bed was what could be called a coffee table.

A rise in this ladies fortunes gave her a larger house to look after, and children to care for. Now her life had become an endless round of chores. Most of these chores are manual—cooking and cleaning then washing then scrubbing, interspersed with cultivating a couple of acres of maize and beans entirely using hand labor. She has no car, no television, no electricity, no secondary schooling, no extensive wardrobe, no flush toilet, no washing machine, no computer, no access to the internet as late as 2014. By this time she was in her mid-50s.

The same lady is everybody's friend. People call by constantly to visit her. Those who come trust her. They talk to her as she cleans, hoes, harvests or cooks. They confide in her, laugh with her, share with her, and the few times it may be seriously needed encourage her. Three of her children live with their families within a mile's radius. More of her six children live within a three-mile radius. Two of her daughters call on her almost every day, often more than once per day. Sons and daughters-in-law are never far away. Grandchildren are around all the time. The same lady is respected and her wisdom is sought out in her church. When she speaks, people take note. Few seem ever to have faulted her straightforwardness and honesty.

There is another lady known to me who once worked professionally. Hence her pension is secure and adequate. At home is a husband, a computer, a TV, electricity, a car in the garage, internet access, an electric and gas cooker, washing machine, fridge, freezer, DVD player, vacuum cleaner, garbage cruncher, dimmable lighting system, stereo player, electric sewing machine, hot shower, numerous choices of soaps and shampoo, plus a level of security such that anyone can walk around outside at any time of night with very little to fear.

This latter lady's closest child is one and a half hours' driving away. When there is rush hour traffic or an accident on the motorway, it could even be more than that. Her children are too busy to just "call by" anyway. Her grandchildren, short of a brief friendly phone call once per month, are far too tied up to relate to their grandmother. As for relating to the neighbors—who are the neighbors? Oh *yes, on one side those people who always seem to threaten to take away this lady's parking space. On the other side is a gay couple who like to display their affection in public. The intensity of this lady's love for children has some neighbors suspect that she wants to abuse them, so they warn their children not to go too near to her. Meetings for fellowship with lady friends are pre-arranged at specific times, and all too often rushed again as no one really has time to relax.*

The two ladies above represent two worlds. They are living out two very different ways of seeking fulfillment for their lives. The way I have presented them, the former seems to be more fulfilled. That would certainly be my conclusion. According to the valuation of the modern western world, she has nothing. Certainly she is vulnerable to all kinds of calamity. Statistically speaking her life expectancy may not be very high. The medical system around her is diabolical, and there is no immediately available vehicle to rush her to where she would receive any required attention. She has no pension. Even if she was "rushed" to hospital, the hospital staff aren't likely to get excited by yet another old woman with a spiritual ailment being brought for them to treat medically. (Whereas western medicine is based on assumptions about the reality of the material world, African medical practice tends to try to deal with the action of non-material agents such as spirits and witchcraft powers.[35]) "Hospital" can even be said to be a misnomer, when most of the hospital staff themselves are convinced that true relief from the ailments their patients suffer from would arise from appropriate prayer and sacrifice. Yet the wealth in relationship that she enjoys is phenomenal. Is wealth of relationship greater than wealth in material?

What happens when these two ladies meet? The second lady is likely to be horrified to find that the first lady sits alongside her charcoal stove on the floor while cooking. The second lady could be horrified to find that the first washes clothes by hand at the riverside. The room she cooks in can fill with smoke. She has no car! When it gets dark she has to get by with very dim-level lighting. She has B.O. Housework takes forever. After dark she won't deign to walk more than one hundred yards from the safety of her home. How does she get by without a computer? The only news she gets is through an old radio with worn out batteries. Her grandchildren's clothes are worn, tatty and old. There is urine all over the toilet floor. That is horrible!!!! She is very poor. According to the second lady, she needs lots and lots of money in order to build a new home, buy a computer, learn to drive, operate a washing machine, use a refrigerator, open a bank account ... you name it. Meanwhile the first lady is rather

---

[35] Harries, *Magical Worldview*, 213.

2. Women in Culture, Equality and "Bi-tegrity"

nonplussed. Surrounded by grandchildren and with as many friends as she ever really wanted, she might wonder what all the fuss is about.[36]

I don't want to seem to be saying that the first lady lives a joyous problem-free life. I am sure she does not. Many things could and often do go wrong for her. Some of her grandchildren have passed away. Calamity might at any time be around the corner. Hence her best strategy is to make the most of what she has. Enjoy the grandchildren. Encourage the daughters. Serve the church. Housework of course does not prevent all of the above. It can even aid it; performing a menial task can help to facilitate conversation. Washing clothes, cooking, laying out beans to dry in the sun, and many more activities can all be done while watching grandchildren and chatting to daughters or neighbors. Time that might have been spent darning the clothes the grandchildren play in so that they not be so torn can instead be used for attending a church fellowship. Every effort being made to live in peace with all and sundry reduces the risk that someone might come to bewitch her. Prayers in the name of Jesus are considered effective against troublesome ancestors.

Painting of the above scenarios might help us to grasp a little of the dichotomy that is set up by influxes of outside money into Africa. I once worked with a missionary who did not realize this dichotomy. He insisted on emphasizing the importance of integrity. Integrity is, according to the Oxford Students Dictionary (2007), "the quality of being honest and having strong moral principles."[37] He wanted African people to be living on the basis of integrity. Meanwhile he was introducing things and ways of working and living from the West that were far from integral to people's lives. Thus he was actively introducing the need for bi-tegrity. That is—the need for two integrities; firstly, integrity to one's own people and ways, and secondly, integrity to newly-introduced foreigners' ways. For example, he did not realize that a part of African "integrity" remains that one does not say no. To him, integrity presupposed the ability to say no. Accepting that one needs a gift and that it will be helpful when one has no means to use it hardly seems to demonstrate western integrity. On the other hand, saying "no" to a gift is undermining African forms of integrity. Outside inputs are introducing our first lady to an alternative system of integrity, one that she does not understand and cannot fulfill. In so far as she does endeavor to live according to that new integrity, she'll be un-

---

[36] What I refer to here is sometimes known as "the American Paradox." (http://www.davidmyers.org/Brix?pageID=21)

[37] As usual, this English language dictionary *presupposes* that there is only one context in which to express integrity, which is a western context.

dermining her original integrity. She is being forced into displaying not integrity but bi-tegrity; one integrity for her donor friend, another for her local community. She is required to please two masters, as it were. Those two masters are vastly different. Integrity has become impossible.

It is hard to find an accurate analogy for the tension that the above inevitably introduces into someone's life. Imagine a bird wanting to peck at food on the ground at the same time as it wants to fly away. Imagine digging a piece of ground so as to plant a maize crop, while having invited local teams to play football on the same field. Imagine trying to control the direction of movement of a car by tuning the radio on the dashboard. Imagine a policeman telling a driver that his fault is that he has no spare tire when he has just been caught driving at 100 mph in a 50 mph limit road. These are all nonsensical combinations. Very often, if not normally, this is the nature of material development assistance as proposed and presented to inhabitants of the majority world. Such assistance cannot be refused. Yet in at least its details it may be largely incomprehensible. Implementation results in bi-tegrity.

I personally instigated some "agricultural development" way back in the late 1980s in Zambia. I very soon intuitively (but not necessarily overtly) grasped enough of the above-mentioned issues to realize that something was going wrong. The scale of my endeavors was not very large. I merely had part-responsibility for the running of the farm associated with the secondary school at which I taught. In addition, through my own interest and enthusiasm, I set out to explore the agricultural practices in the area around the school. Near the end of my three-year stint in Zambia I went out of my way to explore a few agricultural development projects within a hundred miles or so of my home. Wherever I went I seemed to find perplexed African people led by Westerners implementing "development" for them. One project collapsed incredibly quickly once Europeans removed their controlling hand. A vast amount of invested infrastructure representing major efforts by many western experts and donors fast became a ghost-farm.[38] When I went to an agricultural research station, aged twenty-six years with no more than a bachelor's degree in agricultural technology under my belt, despairing African people seemed to want me to take over everything, provide more funds, and turn all the activities around!

---

[38] This was a project by Danish Aid from People to People in the region of Mutanda, North West Province of Zambia. Numerous agricultural projects of all kinds collapsed shortly after Westerners exited. (See also http://www.jim-mission.org.uk/articles/empowerment-or-impoverishment.pdf)

I did not have to venture very far into the local community to realize something about the reception I was getting by local people. That is—that my reception was not conditional on my having a plan or project that made sense in the local context. Instead, apparent criterion that would lead to my popularity hinged on the amount of money I could make available. It seems I could make a great variety of proposals which no one was really going to stand up against—providing I had the money. How was I ever going to get anywhere if that was the extant system of evaluation? I could not find a satisfactory answer. It seemed as if I was coming at right angles to people's sensibilities. How would I ever have intelligent conversations with people about appropriate use of funds when their interests were so at odds with western notions of efficient project implementation and management?

I resolved that part of the way forward must include to relate to people other than on the back of "superior" resources. That way at least, instead of orienting themselves in the way they think will bring the most money, they could be free to tell me the truth.

My example at the start of this chapter is, of course, merely a simplification of the full complexity of the difficulty African people can face as they try to make sense of western initiatives brought into their communities. Whatever may appear simple in terms of people's responses, behavior, and words is not simple in its origins. In other words, African people are not blank slates waiting to be written on by clever Westerners. (For more on this see Pinker.[39]) African people's ways of life are rooted in vast depths of complexity. Those depths of complexity invariably affect the ways in which they respond to initiatives from the West. To Westerners who don't grasp that indigenous complexity, such behavior by African folks can seem to simply lack integrity.

I had the opportunity a few years later to implement my thinking on non-use of resources in Kenya. Two years after my three-year stint in Zambia I moved to Kenya. (For a chronological autobiographical account of my experiences in mission and development work from 1987 to 2012, see http://www.jim-mission.org.uk/harries-bio.pdf.) By the time I went to Western Kenya my interest had shifted from agriculture to theological education. Hence from 1993 I set about teaching theology in a semi-formal extension school in the towns and villages around my home. One barrier to penetrating people's "actual understanding" that I had underestimated was the strength and depth of my identity as a white person in a black African community. As a result of this, even when I said that I had

---

[39] Pinker, *Blank Slate*.

no money, no one would believe me. Now more than two decades later, it is still difficult for many people to even begin to take seriously any notion that I had chosen not to have money to spend on numerous projects. Local people asked themselves: if I had no money, then why I was I there? How can any project possibly succeed without foreign donor funds?

By the time I had spent eighteen years pushing the above extension theological education program, I had met the brick wall of disbelief endless times. My African colleagues certainly did not get it. The prime reason they had any interest in allying themselves with me was on the basis of the presumption that I had access to money. More than the prime reason, perhaps I should be honest and say, often it seemed to be the *only* reason. (Maranz explains the relationship between money and friendships in Africa well.[40]) It was as if my African colleagues had been given a high-grade cow with a large udder. All that anyone could think about on seeing that cow was gallons of milk. Even if the owners said the cow was dry, no one would believe them. To them it often seemed the thought that I might be able to help someone in Africa to "help themselves" other than through accessing foreign money seemed ridiculous.

One symptom of the above was an endless expression of optimism in the face of the direst disappointments: of course, I would get people. Of course it would work. Of course people were keen to know God's word and the Bible. Anyone I met and invited to our classes was almost certain to say "yes, I'm coming." Later, they were not to be seen. Their optimism all seemed to be linked to the presupposition that I must have financial resources to hand out in whatever project I proposed to my African colleagues.

I once attended a center in Africa to which Europeans were regularly invited to come to share theological instruction. As a result of the center having been set up on the back of British interest and money, British people were in most demand. British speakers who came paid their own way, and left financial contributions towards the running of the program when they left. I remained a little puzzled as to why all these intelligent African men would spend so much of their time listening to Europeans tell things that made little sense and were of little direct relevance to their lives. Some African participants provided me with an answer. It seemed they felt free to speak openly using Swahili even when I was with them, presumably because they were unaccustomed to having Westerners with them who understood the language. "The only reason we bring in the British people is because the extra money they bring in is neces-

---

[40] Maranz, *African Friends*.

sary for the financial sustainability of the program," they explained. They went on to add "if it wasn't for the extra money they brought, why else should we bother bringing in and listening to western theologians?" I do not cite their words to declare the end and conclusion of the matter. Those words may not have been heartfelt. It is not good to build theses on overheard conversations. Yet, at the same time, I was amazed to hear the above said. The incentives to dishonesty (i.e., bi-tegrity) that African people are regularly exposed to are so enormous that sometimes one ought to be radically surprised if one ever found an honest (in western terms) African person. Note that my saying this should not be taken as being a slight on African people who, as a result of the behaviors of Westerners, find themselves in impossible predicaments.

So then we have a deeply-rooted system of bi-tegrity. This is a system in which an African person is destined to try to serve two masters: one, their own traditions and ways of life and two, Europeans and their various preferences and demands. Each is followed for the perceived benefits that arise in its own case. As a result, the western system cannot be being followed with "integrity."

3. Language/Culture Conundrums that Lead to Misunderstandings

Discourse about *Roho* churches, such as that at the beginning of chapter 1, reveals a dearth in the English language. Not that English necessarily does not have terms that translate indigenous language words used by *Roho* believers. The terms may or may not be there in a dictionary somewhere. They may even be in English people's heads; but they are not used in routine discourse in English. Neither do African speakers of English know what they are or which English terms to substitute for vernacular ones. This causes a very real dilemma. The same dilemma is often evident when it comes to translation. A listener aware of both languages—an African vernacular and the English it is translated into, can be amazed at how much is left unsaid in an English translation. (For more on this, see Venuti.[41]). [42]

Something akin to the reverse of the above can also happen. At the start of chapter 2, I compared the circumstances of an apparently poverty-stricken African woman surrounded by family with a relatively well-off western woman. Unlike in frequent western language uses, the former does not habitually verbally express either joy at the presence of her grandchildren, nor her love for them. The latter are implicit rather than explicit. There could be many reasons for this. We could say that there are many reasons why a western woman may verbalize her affections and joy. For our African woman things are a little different. First, her role is not challenged or threatened by notions of sexual equality as are grandmas and other "traditional" female roles in the West.[43] Because the role and heart of African grandmas is implicitly understood by all, it hardly needs to be expressed. Secondly, African grandmas may well live in a context in which people live in fear of the effects of witchcraft. Witches typically attack people of whom they are jealous. There is little point in risking provoking the jealousy of others by bragging about one's grand-

---

[41] Venuti, *Scandals of Translation*, 3.
[42] The reverse of course also applies, so that much is lost from translation from western English into African languages.
[43] The notion that a woman might be content in a domestic situation in which she cares for her children and grandchildren is seriously threatened in some circles in the West, where notions of sexual equality imply that she should have and be doing more than this.

children. An African grandma may prefer to conceal the joy she has as a result of being surrounded by her grandchildren. She might not verbalize her love for them. All of the above can give the impression, to a Westerner, that this grandma is less than caring for her grandchildren.

Contextual factors influence the expression of grandmothers' love for their grandchildren. Contexts that determine the appropriate contours of love and care can vary enormously. In many African contexts, threats to life and well-being are of spiritual origin. They are seen to be mediated through witchcraft or ancestral spirits. The nature and prominence of these to some Westerners non-existent entities can help to explain why the behavior of African people can seem "illogical." An appreciation of the nature of witchcraft and of spirits can explain what may for Westerners *appear to be* less than loving behavior towards grandchildren. Because for an African grandma untoward spirits are a hazard to her grandchildren's well-being, pacifying the spirits is a part of expressing love towards her grandchildren. Hence attendance at funerals and other ceremonies that may seem to show neglect to grandchildren, can be more helpfully understood as expressions of love to the same.

The roots of languages used in spiritual churches such as *Roho* churches are assumed to be embedded in mystery. Hence the emphasis is not on understanding how things work, but on ensuring that they work. One indigenous church in Western Kenya has invented a "spiritual language" that is thought to assist communication with the dead. They call this language *DhoRoho*. Hoehler-Fatton tells us how the language is made up.[44] It should be no surprise that language used in churches should be hard to understand, when the whole point is that it is rooted in mystery.

I have already written a great deal about language theory elsewhere. I do not have space to repeat it all here. Given what I have written elsewhere and the insights that I have added above, I hope my reader has realized that a lot of the content of African life is invisible to people from the West. Learning the languages of the indigenous people can help Westerners to perceive hidden content. Languages are best learned while sharing in the ways of life of the people concerned rather than in a classroom.

Failing to appreciate the complexity and invisibility of what is going on can result in the drawing of incorrect conclusions. This can contribute to the widespread view that life in Africa is very simple. Some seem to hold the view that African people are akin to blank slates onto which Europeans are free to write as they please! What the Europeans who so

---

[44] Hoehler-Fatton, *Women of Fire*, xx–xxii.

3. Language/Culture Conundrums that Lead to Misunderstandings

"write" often fail to realize is that words learned in western languages nevertheless acquire a lot of their impacts from African ways of life and languages. As well, as I say, as leaving blank areas in life which exist for Africans but are not visible to Westerners.

There are parts of the belief and practice of indigenous African churches that are biblical, but not recognized or practiced in western Protestant churches. Those western churches usually have very good reasons for not implementing the biblical practices concerned. Because those reasons are almost invariably connected to particular historical developments in their denominations, it can be very difficult to explain them to contemporary audiences who do not share the same history. For example, many contemporary western Protestant traditions do not put a high value on the wearing of particular clothes for church, worship, or prayer. This was a key issue in the Old Testament (see Exod 28). An honest explanation of the whys and wherefores really requires reference to the historical rebellion of Protestants against the Catholic Church.[45] This raises the implicit question—is a lesson in post-biblical church history needed to explain appropriate biblical belief to African people? Similarly—does the holding of "correct" doctrine have to presuppose that believers have passed through a particular history? Can doctrines, such as those regarding the necessity of clerical garb, be accepted as being right for one people, but at the same time wrong for another people? Our main point here is to say that—the biblically authentic issue of the importance of some concerns, such as the importance of clerical garb, while rejected by some western churches, is taken very seriously by some African churches.

Similar in some ways to the above is the question of dreams. Developments in western philosophy in recent centuries have produced a strong and often dominant orientation to positivism.[46] The latter holds that anything that does not have a physical/chemical existence is not "real."[47] Dreams fall into this category. Christians from the West tend to defend "the existence of God," but have often given up in the battle of defending dreams as a means for God to use to speak to people authoritatively in contemporary times. They are apt to accept psychological explanations for dreams. What should they do then when they meet African believers who assume that God speaks to them in dreams? Biblically speaking the African seems to be correct. But according to western peo-

---

[45] http://protestantism.enacademic.com/619/vestments
[46] Mohr, *Christian Origins*, 47 outlines some of positivism's theological roots.
[47] See the glossary for a definition of positivism.

ple including many Christians, dreams can be explained psychologically as arising entirely internally to the mind.[48] That is ironic indeed! I think the clash here is evident. African believers following biblical example have them take the content of dreams very seriously. Western Christians are unlikely to appreciate the value or even legitimacy of this orientation. As a result of this difference, various things happen when the two people's meet. One of these is that, in the interests of seeming to be following contemporary wisdom in the West (where the money comes from), belief in dreams by African Christians can easily go "underground." African believers may well conceal their orientation to dreams from western colleagues.

Finally, there may be content in African Christianity that is a vital part of the life of the community concerned, but apparently absent in both the Bible and in western ways of life. An example of this is the orientation to countering *chira* found amongst Luo Christians in Western Kenya. In brief, *chira* is the curse resulting from breaking taboos put in place by ancestors. It seems to be an unknown quantity in the West. The symptoms of *chira* are similar to those of AIDS (this is another common cause of confusion)—someone grows thin and listless, then eventually dies. Treatment for *chira* is through rituals designed to placate ancestors who have been angered or aggravated. Such rituals often involve the shedding of animal blood. Because of the understood prominence of *chira* in causing misfortune, finding a solution to *chira* becomes an essential and central part of life for many Luo people and so for many Luo churches. Churches cannot afford simply to ignore such a key part of life! Rather, they may be very active against *chira*. That involves them in whole arenas of activity that are unrecognized, and in many ways unrecognizable by the western church.[49]

---

[48] Thus the Concise Oxford Dictionary (1982) defines dreams as a "series of pictures or events in mind of sleeping person."

[49] To my knowledge churches do not practice animal sacrifice as such in the interests of countering *chira*. They may however sometimes condone or encourage animal sacrifice. As African churches can be very overtly active against something called *chira* which is not even mentioned in the Luo Bible (1976), western churches are of course also often very overtly active against aspects of life that are not mentioned in the Bible, for example pornography, pedophilia, violence on television, etc. Some of these concerns may be relatively invisible to African believers.

4. New World Revealed and Its Implication

Our text so far has revealed the presence of a cultural world in Africa that can be very different to that in the West. That world is often concealed from the West, at least in part. Sometimes, even if it is not being consciously concealed, it can still be invisible to the West. Amongst the reasons for its being concealed to the West are those articulated in the prior three chapters. These include: western approaches to race, the almost universal practice whereby Westerners buy their access to African communities rather than taking on "normal" roles in the community, and the widespread use of western languages that by default conceals vast amounts of African culture and ways of life from view. At this point I would like to ask how the presence of this hitherto often unseen world affects the work or ministries that a Westerner may choose to engage in Africa.

There is a kind of acknowledgement of the existence of this "other world" on the part of many Westerners. There is even an acknowledgement of the fact that it has an impact on African ways of life, including on the church. The nature of this impact itself however, being largely unknown to the Westerners concerned, means that beyond acknowledging its presence, they usually do not know how to compensate for it.[50] So they have to ignore it. They expect Africans to appropriate western teaching and to "deal with" the impact of their own culture on "adjusting" what they are appropriating. They perceive that what they have from the West is suitable—given a little tweaking by its recipients (the nature of Westerners' communication suggests that the nature of this tweaking is not of their concern), to enable it to fit into its new African context. To suggest that things could be otherwise, and that perhaps it is insufficient simply to "tweak" western ways of doing things to enable their fit into Africa

---

[50] In using the term "compensate" I am assuming that a known difference between people can be "compensated for" in order to achieve understanding. For example, someone could be helped to understand a colleague's orientation to promoting peace if they realize that he is a member of an Anabaptist church. Knowledge of this church membership is used to "compensate" for what seems to be an unusual orientation. When the impacting context is large and largely unknown, such as the affect of African culture on someone's life and behavior, it is harder for western people to accurately "compensate" for it in their relationship with the African person concerned.

can be quite threatening, if not very threatening. I want to suggest that things are not quite so simple.

Westerners sometimes fail to recognize the extent to which African people have to conceal ways in which pre-existing ways of life interfere with their reception of new things from the West. The reason for this concealment can be very plain on the African side. Any suggestion that their history and traditions could interfere with their appropriation of western know-how can be very threatening to the African individual, and perhaps to a lesser extent their community. *It can be threatening because it seems to suggest that Africans may not be competent communicators of good things (knowledge) from the West to their own people.* In today's world, in which numerous African people are employed, variously subsidized by the West, to promote western ways amongst their own people, this can potentially be a very serious predicament indeed! These people include school teachers, agricultural advisors, policemen, military personnel, government workers, employees of aid agencies, university lecturers and endless others. Must they all be considered to be less than competent in their ability at spreading good things from the West as a result of "interference" from their own cultural backgrounds?

Certain implications seem to follow if indeed the Africa culture seriously interferes with an African person's reception of what is western. One implication seems to be that Westerners themselves need to perform tasks that have long been delegated to African personnel, implying a kind of re-colonization process, and a lot of African redundancy. I suggest that this is actually a misreading of the signs. The communication issue we are looking at arises wherever the cultural chasm is to be crossed, whether or not the Westerner actually does the work with local people on the ground, i.e., whether the Westerners train trainers, or if they train those who will train trainers, etc. *The correct implication of the above is that the "African cultural world" should not be ignored by anybody.* Taking texts from the West and endeavoring to implement them un-translated in Africa is ignoring that "other world." Hence for this and for other related reasons, I suggest that the model of wholesale transfer from the West to Africa is misguided. There is an urgent need for a step of translation to be included in any communication. To facilitate this, it is very helpful for an African country to use other than a European language. *Communication between Africa and the West needs to go through an interpreter.* The interpreter needs to be familiar with both cultures—both the African one and the western one.

One of the problems of bringing the African other-world to the surface is that the conclusion drawn in the above paragraph will not be pop-

4. New World Revealed and Its Implication

ular to everybody. It will be particularly unpopular for those people positively invested in the system that it critiques, which in the short term seems to be most people. Its unpopularity has wide ramifications. Many actions are continually being taken to prevent it from becoming evident. Those actions include attempting to conceal the "African world" from the view of Westerners. Were Westerners to perceive the extent of the impact of the "African world" (sometimes known as the African worldview) on project implementation in Africa and to withdraw their funds, this could in the short-term be disastrous for Africa. In the long-term I would be inclined to say that recognition of the African world is a necessity. Going on running one's lives on the back of knowledge "borrowed" from others is likely, in the long-run, to be the most disastrous.

Ever greater efforts made intentionally or unintentionally to conceal the African world from view present a serious challenge to long-term missionaries and other Westerners working in Africa. African communities are increasingly set up to engage with the physically absent or short-term-only visiting Westerner. Those people are less likely than long-term workers to even perceive the extant depths of difference that there is with the West. When they do hit up against it, they can experience it as culture shock and something to be ignored (particularly if it contradicts notions of racial equality) rather than as learning experience. The long-term worker who acquires a more profound understanding of "Africa" can as a result easily find himself in a pincer trap. One side of the pincer is short-term workers and folks back home who have a strong interest in Africa, but who are not able or do not want to acquire a deeper understanding of cultural differences. On the other side are the African folks themselves who are concerned to conceal (or who implicitly, even if unknowingly, conceal) contextual impacts on their activities, projects, ways of life, etc. The pincer squeezes down on a long-term worker who tries to make sense of the meeting of the two worlds. The pressure of the squeeze can be the most intense when neither Westerners back home nor Africans want to acknowledge the differences that they are experiencing. When both African on the field and Westerner "back home" get together, they can agree to condemn ways in which a long-term missionary is responding to things that they either cannot or do not want to perceive. This is one important reason why missionary and development workers to Africa these days tend to function only for the short term; the above pincer effect ensures that they do not survive to the long term.

Given contemporary habits of communication and the current degree of penetration of globalization, there are essentially two ways for a long-term worker to avoid being jammed into a pincer trap as mentioned above. One is to be careful not to wield power in a way that influences powerful donors or threatens donor-dependent recipients. This is one reason why we have the AVM (Alliance for Vulnerable Mission) recommend that *some* missionaries and development workers (especially those who want to serve for a long time) confine themselves to the use of local resources. In other words: keep their heads down to avoid flak.

The second way to avoid the above pincer trap, the avoiding of which I have suggested above I believe in the long term to be a necessity for some missionaries, is to transform the system of intercultural communication. Particularly critical is to introduce a process of translation into communication where cultural differences are large, such as between the West and Africa. That would happen if an African language(s) replaced European languages in formal circles in Africa. Until this replacement has happened, a visiting Westerner will remain very vulnerable to the pincer movement described above. A long-term missionary who becomes familiar with African as well as European languages and worldviews, can end up acquiring a level of understanding that sees through over-simplistic or absent translation processes in communication going on around him. Because "truth" can threaten vested interests, this needs great care. This is one reason why vulnerable mission by Westerners, i.e., consistently confining oneself to local languages and resources in ministry, is strongly recommended for some workers from the West.[51]

The importance of avoiding acquiring the untoward power that is implicit when one uses a European language in Africa, especially if it is also one's mother tongue, is complicated! Whereas in theory adoption of European languages opens Africa up to the wider world, the presence of the above pincer and other related factors means that it can actually isolate Africa from the wider world. It can also create a lot of unhealthy economic dependence: habituating people to functioning linguistically in other than indigenously-sensible ways, interferes with the kinds of thinking that could otherwise enable sustainability without foreign subsidy. A native-English speaking long-term missionary to Africa is well advised to try to avoid engaging with nationals using English. This means that many conferences, the formal education system, international churches (that use European languages) and so on, can all become "out of bounds."

Just to clarify a little—English itself cannot here be held to be at fault. Theoretically, English could be appropriated and used to promote indigenous African governance. The problem with English however, and this problem seems to grow larger every day with the rise in globalization, is

---

[51] See vulnerablemission.org

4. New World Revealed and Its Implication

that the original owners of English are sufficiently powerful, intrusive, and controlling to prevent African appropriation of the language. The "owners" of English continue to seek to control their language and to use their language to control contexts that they do not understand. The approach to racism taken in the lands that "own" English (that include USA, Australia etc.), that I have already articulated above, illustrates this very clearly: the standard of assessment to which Africa becomes subject is very much western.

5. The Problem of Foundationalism

"Look it is obvious" was a phrase that was in my mind (and probably on my lips) when I went to Zambia to help people improve their agricultural practices. In my early days in Zambia, before I had grasped more of the complexity of what was going on, straightforward ways of engaging in effective intervention seemed to be very evident. In my estimation many development specialists and agricultural and other experts still think in much the same way today; from the West, the needed approach to bringing solutions to many majority world problems can seem to be obvious.

I arrived in Zambia aged twenty-four a few months after finishing teacher training, which I had done immediately after completing my undergraduate studies in agriculture. Having just emerged from many years of schooling, I was oozing with confidence regarding what I knew and what I could do. My years of training (plus hands-on experience of practical farming in the UK and in Germany) had convinced me that I had something of value to share. My going to Zambia to take up my first ever professional position (secondary school teacher of agriculture and co-manager of school farm at Mukinge Girls Secondary School, Kasempa) was finally getting me into implementation phase.

I was one of the "hit the ground running" types. On reaching Zambia, I was excited to see with my own eyes things what I had long thought about and heard about as I had prepared to engage in tropical agriculture. Who would ever have thought that I'd be privileged to one day live in Africa! I rushed into exploration of the school agricultural holdings and into working out what were the likely best "fixes" for its problems. In no time messages went back to the UK "we need hosepipes ... send out seed ... sprinklers is the way to go ... if only we had a modern hybrid species of pig ... enough funds would enable us to build an effective chicken house ... the African people are gifted farmers who are missing just the kinds of insights that I am equipped to provide ..." and so on!

My local African colleagues (the school was Zambian led) did not always "get things" as quickly as, in my view, they ought to have done. That did not discourage me straight away, as I understood that I had a convincing case to make. I struggled on, while of course also slowly learning on the way, for two full years. My Zambian colleagues' opinion of my abilities was perhaps not quite as elevated as my own. All too often they refused to budge from what to me were their insufficiently-thought-through positions. I had to realize that succeeding in getting the school farm to where it ought to be before I left after my three-year term depended on the co-operation of my Zambian colleagues. I asked the mission boss, an American, to come to my home. "You have to tell them to change" I said, referring to my Zambian colleagues. "If they don't change, the school farm isn't going to get anywhere," I assured him. He listened. We talked.

I guess by the end of the above conversation with the American mission boss, even though I didn't realize it in those terms at the time, my faith in foundationalism was gone! My scientifically-grounded education had convinced me that what I was learning was real and true and effective anywhere. I therefore knew that it was transferable, and that I would be able to convince my African colleagues that my understanding was superior to theirs. I thought that I was sure to breach any extant nonsense so as to reach a bedrock of mutual comprehension on which to lay my well thought out (as I considered) ideas. By the end of our conversation I had come to reject a lot of my previous thinking. I determined to work with rather than seemingly against my African colleagues. I determined to listen to them instead of correcting them. Little was I to know at the time just where this new conviction was going to take me. My previous training had included almost no foundation in the social sciences. My Christianity was my motivation for promoting science. I had not intended to ram Christianity down people's throats. My conviction that I was going to work *with* the African people, plus my having to ditch my belief that science is foundational to life, forced me to reconsider the place of my Christian convictions.

I had to do a lot more reading and studying, and pass through a lot more experiences (including frustrations) to get a further grasp of the implications of my new position. More of that story is available here (http://www.jim-mission.org.uk/harries-bio.pdf). Some years later I was exposed to the writings of Plantinga, and thus was enabled to realize more clearly how I had rejected classic foundationalism.[52] To me it seemed that I as a Westerner had in the course of my education been led astray by my own people.

My reader may be wondering just where my Zambian colleagues differed with my own reasoning? Of course the differences between myself and them were and are complex. There was no doubt in my Zambian colleagues' minds that they were correct and that what I was proposing was not sensible. When I look back at my time in Zambia, it often felt like the secondary school under Zambian management was led by children. Strik-

---

[52] Plantinga, *Reason and Belief*.

5. The Problem of Foundationalism

ingly now, after living for many years as part of an African community in Kenya, when Westerners come to Kenya and try and do what seems right to them amongst the African community, they can seem like children. I had to realize that there is no objective foundation on which to build one's knowledge of what is right and wrong, or even of what is better or worse. I began to surmise that the only sort of firm foundation that we had as Christians was our faith in God.

If I am right above, then the question arises as to why the West has become so convinced that it has a unique corner on the truth. I do not have the space in which to make a detailed historical study of this question. I suggest that this is connected to the historical impact of the Gospel on western society. The basic truth of the Gospel message underlies a great deal of what is these days known as European identity. European people have for many years drunk deeply of the Gospel of Jesus. This faith in Christ empowered and built confidence. The knowledge of an all-powerful living God can result in enormous conviction regarding the inherent rightness of one's actions. It often results in feverous efforts at spreading faith in Christ to others. It seems to me that some of the momentum of the fervor that once lay behind spreading faith in Christ, has been transferred to a zeal for thinking founded in philosophies such as positivism, that is expressed in the promotion of secularism.

What may in the future be seen as having been a very shallowly thought through transfer from confidence in God to confidence in realist philosophies is not yet very widely evident in contemporary western society. For the two belief systems (faith in God versus faith in positivistic philosophy resulting in uncritical realism) to be considered to be alternatives may strike some western people as ridiculous. Yet, positivism is totally discredited by the slightest evidence of "spiritual presence." Positivistic philosophy must presuppose an absence of divine powers which it can never prove and for which there is no evidence. The Christian faith, being a belief in the presence of something and not the absence of something, is less vulnerable to being undermined. God might always be hiding where people are not looking! Positivism is therefore a speculation on something that is highly unlikely and impossible to prove,[53] whereas Christian belief is a constantly re-affirmed subjective certainty. This means that anything built on the back of positivism, which includes a significant amount in contemporary life in the West, is very liable to being totally discredited.

---

[53] One could say, for which there is no direct evidence.

So then, why do we see so much confidence in positivism? People like faith that works for them. It is sometimes said that this is especially true in Africa: some Africa churches can be known as "problem solving" churches. (See for example Lado[54]). African people want to believe in something that will provide them with wealth, heal their diseases, and resolve their conflicts. When they find what does this, they latch onto it, sing its praises, and proclaim its truth. I sometimes ask myself whether a parallel thing has not happened in the West. That is to say, as the African pulls out all stops in praising the benefactor or ancestral spirit who is considered to have resulted in the particular prosperity being experienced—has the same not happened in the West with respect to the realms of positivism and science? In both cases the prosperity which has made someone so grateful, may not be associated with the presumed certainty over that which brings it.

The outcomes of scientific research can be mesmerizing and even intoxicating. Their impact on daily life is constantly and everywhere evidenced. Their contemporary impact on human thinking seems in some ways to parallel previous generations' claims of experiencing divine intervention. *That is—the acclaim given to science can seem to parallel praise once accorded to God.* Science is rooted in a kind of temporary amnesia regarding belief in the divine. Temporary shelving of thoughts on divine causation can open up new vistas of understanding.[55] Continue to shelve the divine and yet more incredible insights come to light. The amount of knowledge acquired through an accumulation of scientific research over many generations has today reached enormous proportions. The computer seems to be enabling this to continue to grow almost exponentially! Science can be so exciting as to have us neglect to think of other things. It is as if as a result of this, some people resemble children who are so carried away by the excitement of their own play that they have forgotten the game that they are involved in. It is like youthful vigor that has children forget that they have elders (parents and grandparents) who they will one day resemble! The same elders who were once like them were forced to realize the temporary nature of their once youthful state. Wise youths enjoy what they have while realizing that there is more to life (Eccl 12:1-5). Wise scientists ought to do likewise with respect to the mesmerizing impacts of science. They should realize that there is more to

---

[54] Lado, *Roman Catholic*, 18.
[55] Because such shelving arises from particular interpretations of monotheistic teachings, I consider secularism to be a branch of Christian belief, albeit heretical.

5. The Problem of Foundationalism 51

life. Unfortunately not all do so. Some take science as discrediting Christian belief, a position which Richard Dawkins seems to exemplify. Although from the title of a recent book, it seems that even Dawkins has ventured into the realm of magic and wonder.[56]

The depth and spread of the above deception is astonishing. Following its logic, governments can claim to be secular, social studies claims to be scientific, anthropologists claim to be non-religious,[57] science at times claims to answer moral questions, the authority of foundational scriptures such as the Bible can be rejected on account of their being non-scientific, and so on. All this is having a rapacious impact on western society. Western society was once concerned to proclaim the nature of the God of the universe. Now, as a result of a misguided faith in science, has it become a global movement for nonsensicality? Bit by bit the West, empowered by the supposed foundations in science that also render it blind, are taking apart and throwing away pieces of age-old tested wisdom in favor of shallow supposedly a-theological notions of justice, freedom and equality.[58]

A sufficiently broad analysis of contemporary society might indicate that the once-anticipated scientific utopia is a dying dream. Despite this, the momentum of this dead faith continues. Many western people are reluctant to let-go of their (unfortunately ungrounded) utopian faith in science. I cannot go into all this is in detail in this short text. A recent ruling by an Australian judge that incest may soon no longer be illegal[59] is just one example of the potential impact of unbridled secularism. The contemporary permissiveness to homosexuality seems to arise from a similar root. The attempt at neutrality towards more destructive restrictive ideologies such as Islam that are wearing Christian mantles of "religion" is another. (For more on this see chapter 1).[60] Crediting science with teleol-

---

[56] Dawkins, *Appetite for Wonder*.
It seems that only a small proportion of self-acclaimed atheists consistently express and live out their acclaimed belief. Some are atheists while at university, but no longer so once they get home (Thomas K. Johnson, e-mail message to author, May 5, 2015).
[57] For more on this see Larsen, *Slain God*.
[58] Anthony, *Genealogy of the Western*, 30.
[59] http://www.telegraph.co.uk/news/worldnews/australiaandthepacific/australia/10958728/Australian-judge-says-incest-may-no-longer-be-a-taboo.html
[60] There is an important sense in which the label of "secular" is a means of evading the enmity and aggression of Islam. Nowadays known as "another religion" contemporary to Christianity (thus adding to notions that there is apparent similarity between the two "religions") which Islam is determined to overthrow, Islam

ogy and moral reasoning has put wolves into sheep's clothing. It has fooled masses of Westerners into thinking that doctrinal beliefs and the practices of different "religions" are largely immaterial to the progress of human society. God's eternal plans for the human soul are for many no longer even considered a legitimate talking point.[61]

Drawing towards a conclusion to this chapter, we can say that the West's love affair with foundationalism, while it has brought some benefits of science, has at the same time been destructive. The resulting momentum still coming from its now discredited logic continues to set an unsteady reeling future course for mankind. That is not to say that "God has failed." Rather we can say, biblically speaking, that man has yet again failed to live up to God's expectations,[62] something which he tries to justify with shallow rhetoric. Yes, science has caused a lot of excitement and benefit, but the age in which science and positivism have got an edge in human affairs over issues concerned with the identity of God will most likely in the future be seen as a small blip in the total historical course of mankind. That is, like a short space of time during which peoples' natural intelligence had been overcome by deceptive hollow materialistic philosophies.

The presupposition on the side of the West of the existence of a foundation to life other than God (however defined) has had no small effect on international relations between the western world and the majority

---

is foundationally anti-Christian. The Koran itself contains anti-Christian rhetoric, which many Muslims take very literally. Calling the West "secular" instead of "Christian" is supposed to deflect some of the venom of Islam's attacks. Unfortunately, some people in the West have misunderstood this strategy, as if it implies that the West can somehow put-off the Christian identity that has formed it. (I mention this history of the term secularism not because I have found reference to it in the literature, but rather because it seems obvious that the term secularism would often be preferred to Christianity for the above reason.)

[61] With reference especially to the educational system in America, Marsden tells us that: "If a professor talks about something from a Marxist point of view, others might disagree but not dismiss the notion. But if a professor proposes to study something from a Catholic or Protestant point of view, it would be treated like proposing something from a Martian point of view." (Marsden, *Outrageous Idea*, 7.) On similar lines Beckwith tells us that "academic and media elites treat the church's point of view as if it were an irrational outlier to contemporary culture." (Beckwith, *Faith, Reason*.)

[62] The biblical account makes frequent references to mankind's failures at living up to God's expectations in ancient history. Particularly in view are Israel's failures to meet expectations arising from the Mosaic law and prophets sent by God.

5. The Problem of Foundationalism

world. It has made it difficult to achieve mutual understanding. The West has in recent centuries been convinced of the value of a supposedly positivist approach to life. It has, for some very good reasons, been very hard to convince others of the legitimacy and relevance of such positivism. To people who have not gone through the peculiar history of Europe profoundly influenced by the western church—positivism can be fundamentally senseless. Other people realize what the West seems for a while to have forgotten: a great deal of life is unknown and unknowable in the absence of divine intervention, i.e., intervention from a realm that is beyond the bounds of positivism.[63]

At the start of this chapter I described my experience on a secondary school farm in Zambia. That experience brought things to the surface that are widespread in western intervention into development in Africa. The scale of my engagement with development intervention into the majority world was geographically and economically small—a secondary-school farm. But the basic parameters were there, that are also found in large-scale interventions. The secondary school community in which I worked was a microcosm of endless other often much larger patterns of impact by intervening foreign bodies. The outsider (in this case myself) had already worked out their approach on the basis of assumptions about life that are basically positivistic—that assume the non-relevance of spiritual or divine intervention. Meanwhile, the people I was trying to convince about my case one could say (although the English language here has serious limitations) assumed and observed all causation to be spiritual. Is it any wonder that I appeared to be talking nonsense? A yet greater irony though is that the very people who might have thought I was speaking nonsense are a part of a community that has taken the English language and essentially the British educational system as the preferred foundation in life for all their citizens almost lock, stock, and barrel. As a result, and this is a cause for much confusion today, much of African education is supposedly built on the very presuppositions of positivism that African people themselves often see to be pointless.

The latter seems to be a puzzle indeed. Why educate your people using a system of understanding that does not make sense? The answers in a way are straightforward. In another way they are complex. To begin with something a little more complex, we need to remember that the level of material development of African societies prior to colonial and missionary intrusion was very low indeed. By western standards, aside from

---

[63] I am not wanting here to define "divine" except to say that it is other than positivism.

cows and food, people had very little to their name. A woman who lived in a small mud house possessed a skin to cover her private parts and a few cooking pots, maybe an improvised hoe. A man had a spear, a skin to wear, a stool to sit on, and a hoe. The coming of the European was for such people mind blowing. The "things" that Europeans had were to African people endless and astounding.

One important reason for African people not to accumulate wealth was so as not to become the victim of jealousy, which is closely related to witchcraft.[64] Unlike many African folk—Europeans seemed not to fear the jealousy of others that resulted from their having a lot of wealth. New possibilities of material bounty opened up by this apparent defeating of witchcraft were enthralling to many African people. They wanted it. From very early in the colonial era, they must have realized that it came easily to people who spoke European languages fluently. Therefore knowledge of European languages became a highly coveted commodity.

Closer observation reveals that it is not the use of English that overcomes jealousy. It is true faith in God and his son Jesus Christ that has this effect. As a result there is, in a community bound by witchcraft such as many communities in Africa, a flip-side to English's being so coveted.[65] That is—that people become jealous of those who are capable in English. One outcome of such jealousy, and I believe this is a common phenomenon for people elsewhere and not just in Africa, is that someone using English (or another European language) can make others feel inferior. Use of English, especially if another alternative mutually-comprehensible language is also known, can seem to be motivated by pride. As a result of this plus other associated reasons, African people who use English amongst themselves can appear to be showing off. Someone using European languages in contexts where it is not necessary can be derided. For this and other reasons, the same language that is the language of choice of African policy makers at the same time often has to be avoided. This is just one reason why attempting to swamp Africa with European languages needs constant outside input, generous foreign funding, and in the end cannot be the solution to Africa's language issues.[66]

---

[64] Harries, *Witchcraft*.

[65] English itself, although associated with Christianity and influenced by Christianity is not Christianity. Mechanisms found in Christianity that minimize jealousy of those who are Christian by those who are not, are not effective in preventing jealousy of people who have superior knowledge of potentially lucrative languages such as English.

[66] There are other reasons, including that English in Africa easily becomes "corrupted" by the inclusion of vernacular language words, pronunciations, idioms,

5. The Problem of Foundationalism

Going back a step, we have said that from early in the colonial era European languages became languages of money and wealth. That essentially continues to be the case today. The prominence and attraction of material wealth continues to be the boost or at least a major boost to the valuation of European languages. Sometimes sheer necessity forces this to override concerns of "understanding" or "comprehension" of what is being communicated. That is to say, given a choice of ignorance and wealth or informed wisdom and poverty, most people will, for very good reason, prefer the former. The reason for this choice seems good in the short-term. In the long-term, it results in a society being built on a perilous foundation, something that can have serious ongoing ramifications.

All of the above are no doubt part of the landscape that Alexander explored in the course of his research on the language question in Africa.[67] Alexander noted that powerful languages are almost all, right across sub-Saharan African, European languages. He found that the equation of power was such in pre- and then also post-independence times, that there could really be no other way. That is, the interests of political actors in the period of African independency were such that they effectively had no choice but to choose to govern their countries and perform formal functions using European languages. This links in with arguments I have already made above. Colonial powers, while drunk on the extraordinary powers that positivistic/scientific thinking gave them, at one time considered their subjects in Africa to be less than human.[68] Their intention was not to enable improvement to existing African ways of life so much as to replace them. That left little justification for use of the languages of the people they found. Independence of African states under African leadership was not considered to be a serious option anyway even as late as the 1950s.[69] Hence all eggs were laid in the European language basket. The colonial structures built on European languages were

---

grammar, impacts and even flow! I do not have space to consider all the disadvantages of the use of European languages in Africa here. For more on swamping Africa with European languages see Djité, *Sociolinguistics*, 11, already cited above.

[67] Alexander, *English Unassailable*.
[68] Young, *Colonial Desire*.
[69] The speed with which African countries achieved their independence surprised many. " ... nobody could have predicted that within 15 years of the [1945] meeting in Manchester, the vast majority of African countries would be independent. In the early 1950s, Julius Nyerere, later President of Tanzania, estimated that complete independence would not happen until the 1980s." (http://www.bbc.co.uk/worldservice/specials/1624_story_of_africa/page3.shtml Accessed August 18, 2014.)

the sources and foci of power that leaders of newly independent states could inherit. Politicians who failed to struggle for their control using European languages were simply side-lined, and left without any serious political clout. European languages won the day—almost everywhere.

British and other European powers eventually realized that non-European people who had learned European tongues could confound some of their laudable endeavors, and use their knowledge of European languages to assist "in the anti-colonial struggle."[70] Times changed back in Europe. Notions of racial inequality in which Empire had been built, were being displaced by belief in racial equality. The swing from seeing black people as some kind of non-people to acknowledging them as fully human has come with its own momentum. The opposite swing resulting from this momentum at times blinds contemporary scholars from seeing any differences at all between European and African people. Or if they do see "difference," they cannot afford to mention it or respond to it. Handover of power to Africans, that had just a few years previously seemed totally nonsensical if not impossible becoming a pragmatic necessity, forced politicians and scholars together into a sanctified naivety. From having considered indigenous rule as having disastrous potential consequences, the powers that be had to re-frame it as a positive move in everybody's interests. The effects of this re-framing, intended to engender the faith of people in the potential of the new situation, continue to reverberate to the current day.

The above naivety of handover of power linked arms with the naivety of positivistic thinking to give a facade of credibility to an impossible task. Considering life as a materially-led process of cause and effect in the physical realm helped to remove some complexities from view. The powers that be in Europe presumably tried to do something similar to what I tried to do at the secondary school farm in Zambia (see above). They hoped that holistic African people (for whom traditionally the distinction between physical and spiritual processes is far from clear) would be convinced by their transparent thinking and clear scientific logic. Then the handing over of power at independence could be made to appear to be a technical process that enabled western-trained citizens in Africa to take over European-designed processes. The latter are after all (so it was made out) simply and fully rooted in straight forward common-sense (rooted in positivism) that anyone, African and European alike, should have no trouble grasping.

---

[70] Brutt-Griffler, *World English*, 65.

5. The Problem of Foundationalism

This myth of scientific foundationalism continues to be widely believed in the West today. Those who believe it have had the audacity to set themselves apart from millennia of human history, considering themselves to be some kind of super-race with access to super-knowledge. Such is evident in the very structures of contemporary English (as used in the West) which renders English less and less suitable as a medium for intercultural communication with non-dualistic people such as many Africans. In contemporary English, for example, secularists continue to consider themselves to be founding all that they do on some eternal solid foundation. Others who do not share that high opinion of their foundation are relegated to the status of being "faiths." That is, the prominent notion that is to be presupposed in contemporary English is that there are people who do things on the basis of certainty who are the secularists, and others who live on the basis of *faith* who are religious. Such distortions, that invent gods of material and ignore epistemological reality, are part of the ongoing myth of material foundationalism that continues to (mis)direct western society, and in turn through globalization the rest of the world.

That belief in material foundationalism is erroneous does not in itself make it all bad. Many of its roots are deeply, even if these days invisibly, embedded in Christian truth (in effect in Godly foundation). Divorcing the associated philosophies from their epistemological origins unfortunately has the effect of compromising the possibility of the benefits of the foundationalism from spreading to virgin lands. That is to say—that benefits of the perception of reality that come about from positivism are benefits that arise from an understanding of the nature and power of God taken to a selfish extreme that no longer carries interculturally. The Christian Gospel is a universal message. The positivist gospel is not. Both are rooted in "faith," and in fact in the same faith. The effective carrying of the messages concerned requires an articulation of the same Christian faith.

The lands and people who are these days enthused about development intervention into poor parts of the world are essentially the historically Christian nations. Their orientation to development therefore has grown out of particular theology(s). Contrary perhaps to the view of some, however, theology is dynamic. That is to say—God must be understood afresh by every new generation. The work of a theologian is never completed. As language itself is constantly in dynamic flux, so the nature of God has to be restated for every era and context. Contemporary thinking about how to "do development" is rooted in theological foundations that are now *dated*. People who want to do development, in order to bring depth to their art, also need to be theologians (or at least consult theologians). Development practitioners who do not consider the theology underlying what they are doing are not considering the foundations out of which their actions arise. That is, they are lacking depth in their understanding.[71]

Contemporary development intervention and all that goes with it is very strongly rooted in positivistic thinking. There is a serious need to reconnect development thinking to its roots in Christian theology. Doing so is likely to undercut some of its positivistic nature.

---

[71] The point that I make in this paragraph is similar to one that I have already made in chapter 1.

6. Sin and Life

This text explores the dependence of human life and the thriving of human communities on intervention from beyond the realm of the physical and the material. It suggests that human life can never be entirely rationally grounded. The question of dependence on divine intervention is considered in two ways. One, whether a role for the divine was essential in a particular moment in human history but is no longer essential. Two, whether the need for divine intervention is ongoing. In other words, does prosperous human living require ongoing continuous impact from the divine, however defined, or could it be that divine intervention was required in history to set a foundation that can now function "mechanically"? People who hold the latter view may argue that although our forefathers might have been dependent on insights from the divine, we are now in a post-religious world and can happily go forward on the back of received momentum.

I find the latter view, that we have no ongoing need for the divine, to be rather selfish. It can be equated to kicking away the ladder. If the West got to where it is as a result of the Christian faith but it now no longer promotes the Christian faith, is this not kicking away the ladder, or at least concealing the ladder? Ha-Joong Chang tells us that "the developed countries did not get where they are now through the policies and the institutions that they recommend to developing countries today."[72]

Note that the perspective on the majority world found in this text is different from one that would be rooted entirely in the West. The secular West's efforts at promoting development these days tend to ignore the Christian Gospel. Many parts of the majority world have avidly embraced the Gospel. Those who do such evidently perceive a need for it in their own communities. Seeing faith in God as a kind of outdated evolutionary "stage" in the development of human communities is a misleading anachronism that the West needs to ditch.

The need for divine intervention in human community life, using "divine intervention" in a broad sense of the word, is to me very clearly necessary.[73] I want now to explain this. Essentially, this observation is

---

[72] Chang, *Kicking Away*, 2.
[73] Questions here revolve around the meaning of "divine" in our discussion. See Johnson, *First Step*, for a case for the need for natural theology to be the foundation on which Christian theology is subsequently built. "Human life is a continu-

rendered legitimate by the undermining of foundationalism. In other words, if one removes what Plantinga calls classic foundationalism from the scene,[74] then we get back to a position of having to acknowledge a place for divine intervention in setting a foundation for human affairs.

I think we can all acknowledge that much of the direction we need for our lives is not evident in the physical world around us. Imagine waking up in the morning in a forest or bush/desert, i.e., a place that has been "constructed" by nature rather than by people. You are lying there on the floor. My question is—how do you know what to do without drawing on that which you have inherited from the human community that has reared you? You may be able to stand up and walk, but you won't know where to walk to. You may be hungry—but you don't know where or how to get food. Then you see a beautiful woman. You find her attractive. I am not sure whether you know to distinguish if she is your sister that you should leave her alone, but if not your sister that you are permitted to respond to your instincts and approach her? When it rains you may have the sense to take your wife under the shelter of a tree, but I am not sure that you will have the sense to know how to build a structure for protection from rain or sun? In reality, an enormous amount of what we do and how we do it we inherit from the human community into which we are born. That is, we acquire essential knowledge about life from "spirits," in the sense that a living thing is that which has a "spirit."

We have above acknowledged our dependence on spirits (other human beings) to teach us things that they have somehow learned (or been "programmed to do") in their history. I would like us to consider some rudimentary epistemology. A human person living in a developed community tends to be aware of a way, or a limited number of ways, of doing something. Often that person implicitly considers that the way that they are doing what they are doing is the best way, or even the only "correct" way. This is why moving between "cultures" results in a shock: other people do things differently, but may not necessarily thereby be wrong.

Amongst the reasons people do things differently is that not everything that we do can be calculated on a rational basis. (Hence of course the undermining of foundationalism.) Instead, many of the contexts that people face and in which they have to make choices do not necessarily reveal one clear option for action. There may be many available choices! For a couple sleeping together—who sleeps on which side? Should one

---

al wrestling match with God and his created order, regardless of the belief or unbelief of a person or culture" suggests Johnson.

[74] Plantinga, *Reason and Belief*, 62.

6. Sin and Life

take the short but slippery muddy route to the water hole or the long but dry and more amenable route? My wife has upset me, should I beat her, or should I simply forgive her? My son's arm has become blue and swollen; what should I do about it? (I must make a choice that precedes the results of double-blind scientific trials.) I could pour cold water on his arm, I could add some skin-colored paste to reduce the appearance of blue, I could constrict his arm to stop it swelling, or I could seek to determine which untoward spirit has caused the problem in the first place, and so on. Should I shell the maize in the field so as to make it easier to carry it home, or should I carry it home as it is so as to shell it in the more amenable environment of my home? People regularly come across many, many choices for which there is not one clearly preferred option.

Answers to the above questions are not written into the natural world. They therefore have to come from beyond the natural world.[75] They have to come from, let us say, the realm of spirits. That is, the realm of competing thoughts, disagreement, difference, opinion, precedent, previous experience, example, prior choices already made, and even accident. Those competing thoughts and opinions left to their own devices will result in nothing but chaos. For there to be human community, there needs to be a basis for decision making. That basis has to come from some authority. That is, it has somehow to be chosen and to be legitimated in such a way that it can be more widely accepted. When rationality is not an available basis on which to found such unity, then gods or spirits are the only alternative.[76] Various gods and spirits give different forms of advice. Hence people who follow different courses of life are identified as being those who follow one or other of the various available spiritual paths. These are sometimes known as different "religions."

Some of my readers may be concerned that in the above I am understating the "reality" of God. I probably share the same concern myself. I would remind myself, and that reader, of the philosophy that we are in this text undermining. That is, the previously widely presupposed position that "all that there is" can be divided into the real and the other than real or the unreal. This is the dualistic way that I was brought up to believe in, from my childhood in the UK. We have discovered above that this way of thinking has been undermined. We should also be aware that not everyone in the world holds to that same way of thinking. I propose in this text that the same way of thinking is not necessarily capable of

---

[75] Rowan Williams alludes strongly to this in his recent lecture (Williams, *Representing Reality*.)

[76] I say the "only" alternative, by defining gods and spirits as the alternative.

spreading itself by itself. That is to say—it is not necessarily rationally clear to all people that they ought to adopt western dualistic rationality. Even the wide spread of the western educational system has not instilled this everywhere. Instead, the foundations of dualistic rationality are to be found in Christianity, not in science.

Because not everyone in the world holds to the dualistic distinction between the "real" and the "unreal," neither are their conceptions of God founded on the same distinction. For many people in the world today, and certainly for many people in the history of the world in the past, the question of whether "god" is "real" or "unreal" is absolutely mute. Instead we need to say that for them everything else being real means that God is real, or everything else being unreal means that God also is unreal. One cannot have a category of unreal without a category of "real," so then we are left acknowledging that God is real. This is not a back door means of providing a proof for the existence of God, as others have done in recent centuries in Europe.[77] It is rather stating that, once we have laid aside dualism, God cannot help but to be real because there is no alternative category in which he can be put!

Rozin and Nemeroff take a very different approach to our concern, but can also help us to better understand it.[78] Rozin and Nemeroff were surprised to find much evidence of implicit belief in magic even in "modern" North American students and youth. They point out that the view of disease being related to a "magical" contagion preceded germ theory.[79] If the idea of contagion did not come from an understanding of germs, then where did it come from? Presumably from some "decision-making" way back in the history of humankind. Scientifically speaking, we would have to say that such decision-making was arbitrary. That is, to use Rozin and Nemeroff's term, on the basis of perception of magic. Yet it has provided us with the foundation for germ theory, that is supposedly scientific. Magical beliefs, then, have provided a foundation for science and belief in physical contagions like bacteria. Were those magical beliefs not to have been held, one could suppose that neither would bacteria have ever been discovered. The same laws of magic "are factors in decision making in US culture."[80] The process of discovering science through the means of "magic" seems not to have ended.

---

[77] http://www.philosopher.org.uk/god.htm
[78] Rozin and Nemeroff, *Laws of Sympathetic*.
[79] Ibid., 218.
[80] Ibid., 229.

6. Sin and Life   63

Putting aside the philosophical distinction between "real" and "unreal" undoes many or most of recent debates in western philosophy, especially regarding the existence of God. It is gods who direct human affairs. The critical question which remains is: which god(s) is one to follow? There are many misleading gods, Christians say, who set out to deceive. Yet there is only one God who is truly God, who created heaven and earth, whom we should follow and whom we should glorify. How do we "know" this? There is no other way to know it except; that is what he said we should do.

Western people who discover that I have spent many years living closely with African communities often ask me whether I think spirits are "real." My response is usually to question whether the category of "real" through which they want to define spirits is a legitimate one to use. Hiebert tells us that the terms *realis* and *realitas* were thirteenth century inventions.[81] The Bible as interpreted according to pre-thirteenth century notions of being, presumably does not take any account of the question of the reality or otherwise of gods or spirits. Instead, it concentrates on discussing their activities and their nature. While the question of the "reality" of spirits may be an important one for followers of recent trends in western philosophy, it may not even be a known question in today's Africa. If a question framed from within one worldview (a western worldview) makes no sense in another, e.g., an African worldview, then it is certainly difficult to provide an answer for the former that will also satisfy the latter.

Hiebert encourages us to take a position of critical realism, i.e., to realize that our ability at distinguishing between the categories of real and non-real is limited.[82] Hiebert is happy to accept that the "real" exists, but questions our ability at comprehending it. A typical African Christian may have more difficulty than Hiebert in comprehending the existence of the "real" in the first place. I would like to ask, if the term real was a thirteenth century invention arising from western philosophy, then what gravity should we expect it to have in today's multicultural world? More specifically: how should a western missionary to Africa, where notions of "real" as against "unreal" are unknown to indigenous thought, deal with such a distinction as used in the West? Is an understanding of thirteenth century western philosophy a necessary prerequisite to having a correct comprehension of life, or to a correct comprehension of the Christian faith? Do we simply assume those in Africa who are not *au fait* with Euro-

---

[81] Hiebert, *Missiological Implications*, 4.
[82] Ibid., 37.

pean history to be "wrong" and needing to be enlightened by the West? If not, then the distinction between real and unreal must be laid aside in use of English that claims to be global, at least for the time being. Such laying aside of critical components of western thought has many implications for scholarship in general, including theological and Christian scholarship in particular. If the distinction between real and unreal is otherwise "wrong" but yet is helpful, then foundational means need to be found to introduce it, that I suggest must of necessity be "religious" and not "secular" in nature.[83] Such means, when found, could be incredibly empowering.

A particular case that I want to look at here is that of sin.[84] I want to make some proposals regarding historical understandings of sin and of taboo. From the Concise Oxford Dictionary we learn that a sin is an "(act of) transgression (especially wilful) against divine law or principles of morality." I suggest that from the dualistic West that has been focused on "realism" (science etc.), sin has increasingly been interpreted in practice as "transgression ... against ... principles of morality" that make sense from a scientific/hedonistic point of view. The starting point from which the West has worked has largely been Christian morality, although this fact is often downplayed, ignored, or even denied. My reference to hedonism is to the notion that the "good" act is considered to be that which brings the most pleasure (or least pain) to the greatest number of people. Loosely defined then, according to modern usage, the term sin is used with reference to wrong actions that reduce pleasure or increase pain, the wrong of which can be rationally perceived. In western nations, "sin" has tended to acquire more prominence than has taboo that is irrational. Hence the seven deadly sins were given wide acclaim in the Middle Ages in the West.[85]

The above-described understanding of sin that separates "sin" from the "taboo" category is clearly a redefinition made since biblical times. Taboo, according to Priest, is in the contemporary West considered to be "an interdiction that does not make rational sense."[86] Douglas refers to "that still-continuing process of whittling away the revealed elements of

---

[83] My reader will understand that although this text seeks in some ways to undermine dualism, the fact that it is being written in English that is built on dualism, means that dualism must at the same time be presupposed in terms of the language being used.

[84] Another version of some of the issues discussed here is already published, see Harries, *Sin v. Taboo*.

[85] NEH Summer Seminar, *Seven Deadly Sins*.

[86] Priest, *Cultural Anthropology*, 32.

6. Sin and Life

Christian doctrine, and the elevating in its place of ethical principles as the central core of true religion."[87] Part of that which has here been "whittled away" is the taboo side of the more traditional notion of sin. In other words, the dictionary definition given in the above paragraph of sin as an "(act of) transgression (especially wilful) against divine law or principles of morality" is inaccurate for modern times in which the notion that sin is a transgression of divine law has been whittled away. Because taboo is the sub-category of sin that is considered to be those condemned actions that are relatively arbitrary (i.e., based on divine law), unlike those that are rooted in clear ethical reasoning, taboo seems to be an unnecessary vestige of a prior unenlightened superstitious age.[88] Sins that don't make rational sense, i.e., taboos, need according to this kind of logic to be quietly ignored. "If this is true," Douglas points out, "it reveals a great gulf between ourselves and our forefathers, between us and contemporary primitives."[89]

A much more extended examination of the whole question of the necessity of "taboos" seems to be warranted. Contrary to what remains a widespread contemporary belief, it seems that human life requires taboo. It seems that if taboos are not stated, then they arise from themselves—perhaps by way of what we these days know as being "politically correct." If I am right, that taboos must be there for healthy society, yet there is no rational basis for their instigation, then this points us yet again towards a necessary role in human society for theology and divine revelation.

The above understanding of "sin" as rational has achieved a great deal of hegemony in western nations. Theologians amongst other thinking people have sought to respond to this hegemony. Theologians who seek to defend the relevance of the Gospel of Jesus do so in the intellectual context in which they find themselves. As a result they have been seeking to defend the contemporary relevance of the Bible through emphasizing its rationality.[90] There are many examples of sins in the Bible that make rational sense. For example in the Ten Commandments—the commandment to not steal, or to not kill, with which few would argue. These are the parts of the Bible that have been emphasized. Theologians have

---

[87] Douglas, *Purity and Danger*, 14. Douglas considers that the undermining of taboo occurred very much in the nineteenth century. Yet, it is clear from the fact that James Cook "discovered" taboo as early as 1777 that the concept had already largely disappeared from the view of western people and languages before that.
[88] See also the account in chapter 1 of the *Roho* church.
[89] Douglas, *Purity and Danger*, 8.
[90] Ibid., 11.

sought to explain prescriptions or interdictions that do not seem to make "rational sense" by arguing for their rationality by more adroit means. Here is an example, a commentary on Deuteronomy 22:10:

> Thou shalt not plough with an ox and an ass together—Whether this association, like the mixture of seeds, had been dictated by superstitious motives and the prohibition was symbolical, designed to teach a moral lesson (2 Cor 6:14), may or may not have been the case. But the prohibition prevented a great inhumanity still occasionally practised by the poorer sort in Oriental countries. An ox and ass, being of different species and of very different characters, cannot associate comfortably, nor unite cheerfully in drawing a plough or a wagon. The ass being much smaller and his step shorter, there would be an unequal and irregular draft. Besides, the ass, from feeding on coarse and poisonous weeds, has a fetid breath, which its yoke fellow seeks to avoid, not only as poisonous and offensive, but producing leanness, or, if long continued, death; and hence, it has been observed always to hold away its head from the ass and to pull only with one shoulder.[91]

I am not claiming that the above example constitutes a "proof." I give it to illustrate a Bible commentary that while considering non-rational as well as rational bases for a belief, clearly comes down in favor of the rational. Jamieson, Fausset and Brown mention possible superstitious and symbolic motives, but come out strongly in favor of an interpretation that seeks to avoid ill health of the animals concerned on a rational basis.[92]

One can only believe that the advocacy of the rationality of Christianity and western life in general, i.e., "the distinction between contagion and true religion"[93] was confirmed by 1777. In that year, the explorer Captain Cook reported on his experience on the island of Tonga. On exploring the ways of life of the people of Tonga, he was "surprised" to discover that unlike Europeans they did not root all of their lives in reason and rationality. Instead, they had a belief in something called *taboo*. Cook's reporting was such as to result in the word taboo entering English and other European languages.[94] It thus entering European languages, strongly suggests that a descriptive term for this concept was at the time absent in European thought. Taboo, prohibition on behavior based on

---

[91] Jamieson et al., *Commentary, Critical*.
[92] Ibid.
[93] Douglas, *Purity and Danger*, 21.
[94] Holden, *Taboos*, 4.

6. Sin and Life 67

other than reason and rationality, therefore came to be defined as something other than in the category of sin, using a term that is not the term sin. Surprisingly then apparently to some, the Bible was later found to contain many taboos![95] Christians naturally (given the circumstances of the day described above) objected to the suggestion that their faith was based on other than what is rational and reasonable. For western Christianity in due course reason/rationality in some ways took pre-eminence over God himself.

I hope my reader will appreciate that the above circumstances resulted in a splitting of the content of the original meaning of the term sin into two categories according to its perceived allegiance to western notions of rationality. Those categories are sin and taboo. The former, sin, was considered important. Its content became enshrined into western legal systems, that themselves arose from Christianity.[96] Hence Holden's contrasting between sin and taboo.[97] The latter, taboo, was condemned as being largely irrelevant and superfluous to life.[98] Anyone, including any Christians, who stuck to notions of taboo were considered backward, superstitious, or primitive. As a result of such condemnation, many Christians sought to defend their faith according to the parameters of acceptability of their communities' standards of rationality. Such defense continues to date under the title of apologetics.[99]

The above basis for defense of faith has had (and continues to have) many interesting and consequential side effects. Amongst such effects is a reinforcing of the belief in dualism between what is "real" (the effects of "real" sins, that make rational sense and have become foundations for rational law) and what is not real (considered to be taboo). It can be argued that the defense of the Gospel as a rational system has distorted New Testament Christianity. It has in turn impacted on missionary work beyond the West. Protestant missionaries especially (less so Catholic, and less so again Orthodox) have spread a faith that has intentionally as far as possible been shorn of non-rational content. It is ironic that such be the

---

[95] Frazer, *Folk-lore*, vii. Here referred to by Frazer as "rudimentary survivals from a far lower level of culture."
[96] Mohr, *Christian Origins*, 37–38.
[97] Holden, *Taboos*, 4.
[98] Contrary to this, Holden points out that taboos "continue to exert their power" in contemporary life (Ibid., 4).
[99] Googling "definition apologetics" the most prominent response indicated apologetics to be "reasoned arguments or writings in justification of something, typically a theory or religious doctrine" (accessed August 19, 2014). (Found in the Oxford Dictionary of Difficult Words, page 27.)

nature of the faith that is shared with non-western people who quite likely do not even understand the West's aversion to what is non-rational. A faith shorn or whittled of its extra-rational content has been presented to a people who themselves would be quite happy with the original extra-rational content. The people are given a faith grounded on principles that they themselves do not hold and cannot understand—i.e., that to them are of the nature of taboo![100] In this case however the "taboos" (i.e., guidelines arising from western rationality) incorporated into Christianity are supposedly not of divine origin but of human origin.[101] Ironically—western Christians have shared a faith the living out of which requires allegiance not only to God but also to them. This has obviously been a major contribution to the issues of dependency, and to prosperity gospel, and to idolatry ("worship" of Whites rather than of God). As well as making people dependent on God, western missionaries have also increasingly made them dependent, for the correct execution of their faith, on Westerners.[102]

The fact that human society is historically rooted in non-rational beliefs is recognized by some. Modernism is after all a relatively recent invention. Modernists see the pre-modern period of history as a time of having been under-enlightened. What they less often consider are ways in which the nature of their "pre-rational history" might have laid foundations that are essential to who they are today, including to the rationality that they have today. Here we link in with our previous topic of foundationalism (chapter 5). If there is indeed no objectively-grounded objectivity out of which human reason has been formed, then contemporary objectivity must have originated from some kind of subjectively-grounded objectivity that should really be considered to be subjectivi-

---

[100] If indeed the non-West accepts the role of the divine in the determination of morality, this presumably means that efforts at founding morality entirely on reason may make little sense to them. So it could be said to be for the non-West a taboo to hold to a faith that has discarded its taboo foundations. Living a way of life that is based on the rationality that is very highly valued by the West could be taboo to those who cannot accept foundations that appear to ignore the role of the divine in the determination of morality.

[101] The very monism, i.e., absence of dualism, in much of the majority world, Africa here being in focus, results in situations like this in which the divide between human beings and gods becomes blurred. The blurring of this divide is very consequential for the rest of this text.

[102] This is, of course, just another way of saying that they have produced a problem of unhealthy dependency on the West. (For more on dependency as a practical "problem" see Schwartz, *When Charity Destroys*.)

6. Sin and Life

ty.[103] In other words—the non-rational would seem to be a necessary foundation for rationality. To pursue this further, we could ask whether a human community that was disconnected from its history but exposed to rationality could thrive, or could become "rational"? We are asking whether rationality is a sufficient basis through which to enable a people who find themselves living in the light of their history to themselves become "rational." (I here use the terms "rational" and "dualistic" somewhat interchangeably.) Or is a component (or components) of the other-than-rational required to enable a people to become rational? I suggest that the latter *is* the case: that a certain foundation in irrationality is a necessary precursor to rationality. This then raises a question mark on the rationality of rationality. If rationality is founded on irrationality, then advocacy of rationality without that accompanying irrationality is pointing people down a dead-end road, thus is immoral.

I suggest that advocacy of rationality can indeed, as suggested above, be essentially immoral. To be true to its roots, rationality, in so far as it is rational, must be accepted and understood as a part of something that is less than and other than rational. Whether or not this latter proposal seems rational, it is nevertheless in the nature of things, and part of the nature of human life. In other words to use contemporary terminology, "religion" is essential to human existence, including to majority world development.

If there is no alternative, as we have found above, but for human life to be rooted in religion, then this raises the question of "which religion?" That is, do all "religions" effectively lay the same foundation? Or does the nature of the religion concerned determine the characteristics of the foundation on to which rationality may be built or out of which it may emerge? If the latter, then the nature of the rationality that will arise is dependent on the nature of the religion onto which it is built. I suggest that clearly the latter is the case, and that there can be no other way. I will come back to this again in more detail below. Amongst the very practical conclusions arising from the above is that the most effective way of promoting a rationality, which is of necessity rooted in a religion, is to promote the religion in which it is rooted. That is to say—if indeed a rationality is dependent on a religion but not the other way round (and indeed so it must be), then the foundational basis for intercultural advocacy should be the religion and not the rationality. The key work of intercultural advocacy is that of the missionary, and the person doing "development" follows in his wake. This is very evident in practice in

---

[103] Arguably, subjectively grounded objectivity is not objective at all but subjective.

contemporary Africa, where countries and peoples that are open to "development workers" from the West are predominantly those that have become Christian.[104]

To go back to the issue of sin—it seems clear that anthropologists amongst others utilized the division between taboo and sin as a stick with which to beat Christianity. Christians in the West were insisting that sin avoidance was a vital part of healthy good human existence.[105] Meanwhile anthropologists began to explore non-western communities. Many if not all of those anthropologists had agendas.[106] Amongst their agendas was a discrediting of Christianity; anthropology has long used "the study of social others . . . to undercut theologians" Priest tells us.[107] Secular anthropology emerged and grew out of a rejection of certain theological positions. Defending itself therefore required anthropology to continue to attempt to undermine those alternative theological understandings.[108] In effect, anthropology implicitly defends a theological orthodoxy that presupposes an understanding of sin that is "rational."

On arriving in non-western communities, anthropologists sought to find out if the latter had notions of sin similar to those in their own communities, i.e., rational notions of sin. If they did not have such notions, then the question that followed was whether people could still be happy and prosperous without them. If so, then it would appear that western people's laboring under the need to feel "guilty" about their acts of sin was unnecessary. The anthropologists indeed found that "lacking the European's sense of sin, such [non-western] people were thought to

---

[104] Because "in contemporary discussions of ways to attain sustainable and authentic human development, there is a reluctance to consider the influence of religion" (Ogbonnaya http://www.saintleo.edu/media/411881/religion_and_sustainable_development_in_africa_final.pdf), this statement is difficult to support from the literature. From general observation, it would seem to be very true.

[105] Priest, *Cultural Anthropology*, 86.

[106] Ibid., 93.

[107] Ibid., 94.

[108] Because anthropology grew out of a particular theological understanding, it could itself be said to be theologically positioned, and so in need to defend itself against alternative theological positions. Anthropologists find themselves needing to defend a relatively narrow theological orthodoxy. As contemporary so-called atheists—anthropologists can become very concerned when the "goalposts" of theological belief shift. Philosopher Reitan tells us how a professing atheist accused him of "redefining religion so that it no longer matches the target that the New Atheists attack, then defending the re-defined religion, and then finally claiming that since redefined religion is so easily defended the New Atheists are therefore wrong." (Reitan, *Moving the Goalposts*, 81.)

6. Sin and Life   71

enjoy a happiness that escaped the guilt-ridden European."[109] Following this, missionaries could be branded as "destroyers of joyful innocence,"[110] and indeed they were so branded. Priest recounts many instances and means through which anthropologists mocked Christians, and especially the Christian missionary. (See especially Priest.[111])

What anthropologists undermined was, of course, actually the myth that liberalists had created and that western Christianity had to various degrees taken on board. That is the myth that considered that all sin, to be considered legitimately sin, had to pass a "rationality" test of approval. That is the kind of sin that anthropologists did not, for some very good reasons that we should be clearly understanding, find amongst non-western communities. The sin that they were searching for had its "goalposts" positioned in certain ways. Had they not been so positioned, then they could not have found it to be absent. What anthropologists were undermining was not Christianity. It was its modern interpretation which supposed that Christianity could be entirely rationally grounded. It is important for contemporary scholars to grasp this critical point. The undermining of foundationalism, described in chapter 5 of this text, has undone a lot of academic work that was at one time thought to be done and dusted. This is just one example of such that requires the undermining of Christianity to be undone.

Anthropologists rejoiced at having undermined the theologians' craft! Not only had it been undermined at home by liberal thinking. It had now also, as a result of the discovery that non-western people could live happy lives without the strictures of the prohibition of "sin," been undermined abroad. I have already pointed to the fundamental error of the liberals or rationalists above.[112] That is—that they assumed (until the mid-twentieth century) that the foundation they were building on was firmly rooted. We now have to question this, and to realize instead that in absolute terms in the absence of an active-deity (God) their foundation was as arbitrary as would be almost any other foundation. So we have seen that far from undermining theology, liberalism, reason, and rationality are building on theology. Far from anthropologists having undermined theology, what they actually undermined was that interpretation of theology that had been built on the same foundation in opposition to which anthropology itself had been built. Christianity is "anthropology's

---

[109] Priest, *Cultural Anthropology*, 88.
[110] Ibid.
[111] Priest, *Missionary Positions*.
[112] See chapter 5.

theoretical repressed."[113] That is the foundation built on liberalism that endeavored to divide the "real" from the "divine" and "sin" from "taboo" and side-line both divine and taboo. By finding that there was no sin apart from the divine, anthropologists had actually rediscovered a necessity for the divine in human existence. Unfortunately (or fortunately?) they seemed not to fully realize this at the time.

The anthropologists' misunderstanding arose from the traditional content of the term "sin" having been whittled down as a result of pressure from advocates of rationality to respect only sin-that-is-rational.[114] When anthropologists found sin-that-is-rational to be absent in non-western societies that they were beginning to explore, they concluded that the category of sin was absent and therefore unnecessary. Had they included other-than-rational content under the broad category of sin, then they would not have found sin to be absent because this (which from the day of Captain Cook came to be known as taboo) was very much present. Hence I have in this text undermined historical attacks on theologians from both rationalists at "home" and anthropologists abroad.

The above case, if correct (as I take it to be), has enormous consequences and potential consequences for contemporary advocacy as to what are good ways of life. The foundation for the reasoning that has been used to undermine the role of religion, specifically Christianity, in the life of people in the western world has above been shown to be spurious. A considerable amount of back-pedaling seems to be necessitated. How will the scholarly world respond to such an undercutting of the supposedly foundational principles on which it has been building? Quite likely of course—by doing its utmost to defend the status quo. Extant paradigms are defended by their adherents until their defense becomes inadmissible.[115] This is the position we are in at this time in the contemporary world. We are, as mentioned above (see Introduction) in a time period in which the undermined liberal/rational/modern paradigm continues on the basis of previously acquired momentum.

A continual shoring up of an outdated paradigm is, I suggest, to put it politely, unhealthy. It is in effect living a lie. It is a spreading of untruth. It is misleading. It is cruel. It is immoral. It is unjust. It can be homicidal. It is illegitimate. Allow me to root some of this condemnation in contemporary reality in terms of the relationship between the first world (the West) and the majority world. Declarations as to progress being made in

---

[113] Cannell, *Christianity of Anthropology*, 341.
[114] Douglas, *Purity and Danger*, 14.
[115] Kuhn, *Structure of Scientific*.

6. Sin and Life

majority-world development are these days many and frequent. (I will concentrate on Africa.) At the same time, observers notice that much so-called majority world development occurs on the back of unhealthy dependencies on western funding and control, which latter according to Bronkema is ever growing:

Today, the foreign aid industry plays a massive role in the economies at the local, national, and international levels. "Hundreds of thousands of jobs depend on it in the north and the south, and it permeates just about every single facet of the life of developing countries. . . . foreign aid actors and resources stand accused of creating dependency and meddling . . . It is in this maelstrom of political economy that NGOs are operating."[116]

The "success" in indicators of development being measured, I am suggesting, is not necessarily at all a result of the "success" of the strategies employed in bringing helpful change to underdeveloped peoples. Instead, what is all too often being measured is the outcome of the "massive role"[117] that the foreign aid industry plays in majority world economies. Those doing the "intervening" are working from the foundations provided by their own particular and peculiar "religious" histories. Because it is the resultant "objectivities" and not the foundational theologies that are gaining pride of place, populations of majority world countries (at least many African countries) may not themselves be being empowered at all. What we have is dependency masquerading as development. What is missing is its religious underpinnings.

Declarations in much of sub-Saharan Africa regarding indigenously-rooted development are, I suggest, being made on the basis of faith. That is though—faith in a system that we have seen above to be effectively defunct (foundationless). At the same time such faith pushes numerous agendas in certain directions. Many of these agendas are appropriated by very powerful global bodies including the United Nations, World Bank etc. Such commitment to the promotion of groundless agendas obviously precludes other alternative agendas from gaining prominence. If the alternative agendas are the ones that can save life, then the promotion of false agendas that prevent them from acquiring prominence can justifiably be considered to be immoral, unjust, and even homicidal in their outcomes.

---

[116] Bronkema, *Flying Blind?*, 226.
[117] Ibid., 154.

7. Finding a Foundation for Life

The nature of the category religion as used in western English has essentially arisen from people's understandings about Christianity. This point is made clearly by Islamic anthropologist Talal Asad. In a discussion in 2009 with Gil Aridjar, Asad tells us that: "my primary point was that the concept of 'religion' has Christian roots, and that in an important sense it is ... a translation of Christianity or ... an abstraction and generalisation of elements regarded as basic to Christianity."[118] According to Asad "a trans-historical definition of religion is not viable.[119] What appears to be self-evident in religion, Asad tells us, is "a view that has a specific Christian history."[120]

One response to an over-broad use of the term "religion" to describe Islam, African Traditional Religion and other "ways of life" as "religions," has been to deny that Christianity is a "religion." "Religions are human searches for God, while God has come to us in Jesus"[121] is something that I have also frequently heard. Claiming that Christianity is not a religion has close parallels to claiming that it is the only religion. In both cases the legitimacy of direct parallel similarity with other "religions" is being denied. In this book I am more inclined to suggest that Christianity is the only religion rather than not a religion, because the term religion has frankly historically evolved as a label to use to describe Christianity (as Asad above).

Following the above, I would be inclined to ask: if indeed the term religion is so much connected to Christianity, is it really legitimate to use it for anything else? This is like asking if it is legitimate to refer to sheep as cattle? Let us say that we have a cattle farmer who understands cattle. If the term *cattle* has been defined according to the nature of cattle themselves, is it legitimate to use the same term to refer to other animals, let us say to sheep? If another person keeps other animals, let us say sheep, our cattle farmer has a number of choices. He could call all the animals cattle. Or he could call his own animals cattle but the other man's animals sheep. Or he could refer to all the animals using another category that is specific neither to cattle nor to sheep, for example, livestock. If he calls all animals cattle he is making a category error, because sheep are

---

[118] Asad, *Responding to Gil*.
[119] Asad, *Construction of Religion*, 116.
[120] Ibid., 122.
[121] Thomas K. Johnson, e-mail message to author, May 5, 2015.

not cattle. Because the category "religion" is modeled on Christianity, that is equivalent to the category error being made by English speakers in the world today who call Islam and Hinduism "religions." An alternative is to acknowledge that those other animals are different, and call them sheep. That is saying that other people's beliefs, for example Hinduism and Islam are different from Christianity (i.e., that sheep are different from cattle), so they do not fall into the category of "religion." To call them "faiths" may be just as misleading, as it implies that they are held by "faith," and that there are other ways of life (e.g., secularism) that is not based on faith. Perhaps an appropriate label for them is "ways of life"?

In today's world some people object to animals being kept by someone else being called by a different name to one's own animals. That is to say: they object to the suggestion that different so-called "religions" are really foundationally different. It is this objection that has forced western society into using a relatively specific term like religion for things that do not "fit" the label (i.e., that are not Christianity). The use of the term "religion" has been a part of the misleading strategy of implying that "religion" is some kind of superfluous extra to the "real" thing which is secularism. It is a term like "barbarian" or "gentile" that implies inferiority on the part of all that is not secularism. It has also implied that choice of religion is of little consequence in terms of the outworking of people's lives. I guess we could term this to be a subtle anti-Christ (1 John 2:18).

Western man looking out on the world situation that was coming to his attention with increases in globalization, did so with a certain perspective. It soon became clear that not everyone in the world knew about the claims of Christ and the traditions that had been built up on the back of those claims. Those in the West who had been convinced by secularism (remember this was the time prior to the undermining of the foundations of secularism) found other people's ways of life, unlike secularism, to be rooted in myths, stories, fables etc. For a secularist brought up in a Christian society, those things (myths, stories, fables etc.) seemed to be parallel to the Christianity rather than the secularism back home. Some other people's myths and fables were rooted in scriptures which western people then assumed must be equivalent to the Bible. Whether or not there were scriptures associated with the people's beliefs, to modern man these "other (non secular) things" seemed to resemble the once but no longer hegemonic category back home called Christianity. Hence modern man developed a label for things based on myth and fables that either were no longer hegemonic or were expected shortly to be no longer hegemonic.

7. Finding a Foundation for Life

He gave this category the label of "religion," and modeled the same category on Christianity.

More recently we have had to realize that secularism/modernism are themselves of necessity rooted in myths and fables. There can be no other way, because without myths and fables one does not get a foundation with which to understand and order life. (See chapters 5 and 6, and Lakoff and Johnson.[122]) Science and objectivity are themselves not grounded in science and objectivity, because there is no available ground called science or objectivity that is either scientific or objective on which they can be grounded. Language and understanding are all far too subjective. In this sense, we have to realize that science and objectivity are themselves facets of "religion," that have grown out of faith in certain "myths and fables," especially in actual fact out of Christianity. So what then with the category religion? It encompasses everything. Except, that is, certain western people (i.e., "secularists") who believe that they have another category which exempts them from the category of religion according to a certain foundation-less myth.[123] When they find parallel beliefs (that they also consider to be "secular") amongst other peoples, then they might consider those also to fall outside of the realm of "religion."

Ironically, the people who have preferred the term "religion" to incorporate other people around the world who are not Christian, are most notably Christians. Christians are after all universalists—they believe that God who they worship is everybody's God. So for a Christian to say that Buddhism is "another" of the same kinds of beliefs that they have themselves is to imply that God loves them as he does Christians. That is to say—Christians may be very happy with the use of the term "religion" to describe what are seen as alternatives to Christianity, because the use of the term seems to draw them closer to Christian belief. (This demonstrates a way in which language is formed theologically.) The problem has come when so-called secularists have misappropriated this understanding. They have spread the understanding that there are other "religions" around the world that all resemble Christianity but are not Christianity, on the basis of their belief that there is anyway "no god," so that all these beliefs including Christianity are anyway only fictitious inven-

---

[122] Lakoff and Johnson, *Philosophy in the Flesh*, 36. Lakoff and Johnson use the term "folk theory."
[123] Welbourn shares my concern on the illegitimacy of the category of religion in stating that "the contemporary isolation of 'religion' as a separate subject of study is methodically wrong." (Welbourn, *Towards Eliminating*, 14). If only a myth separates secularism from religion, then that raises questions of just whether/how secularism can be considered to be distinct from religion.

tions. Another foundation stone for secularists has been the presumption of the essential irrelevance of "religion" to public life. They have taken it as being a private affair that is largely inconsequential publicly. Of course, not to do so is to question their own claim to hegemony—as the new belief that was to have taken over from all religions. (See also Beckwith.[124]) The use of the term "religion" that is designed to fit Christianity to incorporate many ways of life that are not Christian, adds a lot of implicit baggage to people's understandings of "other religions." That is—it makes other ways of life appear (to Westerners) to resemble Christianity. That added baggage, that does not belong where it has been added, spawned and is still spawning numerous if not almost endless misunderstanding. Because these understandings arise in the West and in English scholarship that has been appropriated globally, an apparently small misunderstanding is having enormous global consequences.

A particular area of misunderstanding important to us in this text is clearly the relationship between Christianity and secularism. We will see below that a peculiar feature of Christianity has been its tendency to create dualism(s). One aspect of the dualisms created is that someone can be a Christian, yet be content to be under "secular" rule. The use of the term religion to describe other people's beliefs and practices around the world has carried with it the implicit presupposition that those other people are or should be just as happy to allow secular rule over them, and a demotion of their "religious" practice to a part-time spiritual sphere. Often such a presupposition has been incorrect. The degree to which it has been incorrect continues to go largely unnoticed in scholarship as well as in popular thought.

The content of chapter 6 in this text seemed to leave us hanging perilously over a cliff edge of chaos! In chapter 6 I pointed out that the foundations for majority world development need to be in correct "religion." In doing so, I seem to have managed to undermine much of the "modern project." Then we need to ask ourselves—what is to take the place of "modernism"? I continue to demonstrate below how realizing the illegitimacy of use of the term religion could give us some wiggle room with which to begin to address the above mentioned stalemate in global affairs, including especially majority world development (with a focus on Africa).

Spicer reminds us of a time when Christianity was, in Europe, not considered "a religion" but a necessary truth.[125] It was clearly in many

---

[124] Beckwith, *Faith, Reason*.
[125] Spicer, *Of No Church*.

7. Finding a Foundation for Life

ways considered to be dominant truth—few deigned to undermine or question it. Any who did so could be widely condemned.[126] The rest of life was considered, it appears, in relation to the truth of the Christian Gospel, rather than the other way around. That is to say—adherence to the Christian faith gave the West a foundation on which life could be understood and ordered. This foundation came to be an, if not the, major contribution to the subsequent development of what has more recently come to be known as modern life.

Currents of thought now identified in this text as falsely grounded came to undermine such foundation. I will repeat some of the above argument in different words. That is—realist philosophies that propose that the material world has a foundational role in thinking and understanding have in recent centuries undermined the hegemony that used to belong to Christianity in the western world. Doing so, and having been seen for a number of centuries as having done so with considerable legitimacy, has in much western thinking displaced the hegemony of Christianity with a hegemony that could these days be labeled as *secular reason*. To those who accept the claims of secular reason, Christianity has become a sub-system to the new hegemony. Instead of seen as being rooted in sensibilities, Christianity has to many come to be understood as being rooted in myths, stories, fables, tales and unreliable stories. The developing "modern" world needed a category with which to label Christianity which now was to be considered as a non-hegemonic system. The label that came to the fore for this category was religion. Hence religion came, in the West, to be understood as being a system of beliefs contingent on myth and fable that is subject to and essentially inferior to an over-arching secular hegemony. Religion was the term of choice for Christianity in the newly secularized/modernized world. Now that the foundations of secular modernism have been undermined, we can see that "religion" is a very inappropriate term. If, as has been the case since the mid-twentieth century, it has to be acknowledged that secularism can no longer be considered foundational, the role of being a foundation in life has got to go elsewhere, essentially to something akin to "religion."

We have identified three things about religion above. One, religion really is Christianity. Two, that when extended to and applied to other than Christianity it can be considered an illegitimate category. Three, religion is an unhelpful description for Christianity, at least in so far as it implies that Christianity is secondary to secularism when actually the re-

---

[126] Larner points out how hard it is for contemporary people to grasp this reality, so much has changed in intervening centuries (Larner, *Witchcraft and Religion*, 114).

verse is true. Having considered some of the implications of the problems with the category religion, I now want to consider more of the implications of its co-identity with Christianity. Ironically, Christianity has identified that there is something "real" that is beyond itself. How this has come about has been much disputed. That it has come about is little disputed. For example, Christianity can content itself as a complementary force to a secular ruler, like a king or secular government. In this sense, it has proved capable of producing a dualism. This seems to be traceable to some of the teachings of Jesus, such as "give to Caesar what is Caesar's and to God what is God's" (Mark 12:17).[127] Such dualism, as I alluded to above, allowed for the development of modernism and secularism. This confirms that the latter are therefore really a part of and outcome of Christianity.

Many scholars have at different points made the link between Christianity and the origins of modernism. Marcell Mauss "considered Christianity decisive in the formation of modern Western understandings of the self."[128] A recent study by Robbins *et al.* is perhaps particularly valuable as a way of confirming this.[129] Robbins *et al.* engaged in a comparative study of the impact of mission work on three very different ethnicities from Amazonia and Melanesia. They found that "conversion in all [their] cases radically transform[ed] notions of the inner self, the body, and relations between people."[130] These researchers found that "Christian conversion can lead to substantial changes in people's conceptualizations even of core domains of cultural understanding such as that of selfhood, domains anthropologists sometimes imagine are rarely subject to such profound transformation."[131] If such understandings of self are indeed prerequisites for modernization, and Robbins *et al.* demonstrate that they are acquired as a result of becoming Christian, this gives a further clear pointer to Christianity as being foundational to modernism. The means to assisting people to take advantage of benefits of "modern" life would seem therefore to be Christianity. We have seen that the foundation for modern science cannot be in science. It must be in something other than science. That "something other" is a foundation for living that can restrict its own operations to a certain sphere, thus leaving a gap to another authority

---

[127] I have surveyed different ways in which the Christian Bible takes people in the direction of secularism in Harries, *Secularism and Africa*, 102–135.
[128] Cannell, *Anthropology of Christianity*, 1.
[129] Robbins et al., *Evangelical Conversion*.
[130] Ibid., 585.
[131] Ibid., 587.

7. Finding a Foundation for Life

that is not it but is nevertheless under the ordered command of a mighty God. I do not have space to go into all aspects of the implications of this in more detail here.

There is a very important issue to be considered here relating to the role of Christianity in setting the foundation of science. Science seems to work. Scientific innovations have in today's world transformed the lives of billions of people. The transformation continues. How can this be, we might ask, if as we have also discovered, science is not capable of putting in place its own foundations so must be founded in belief in the divine? Could the foundation for scientific discoveries have been built entirely on chance, or must building it have involved the intervention of an intelligent being? If what we have identified as the necessary "divine" input required for the development of modern science is actually "chance," then it would seem that the chance of science "working" would be very slim indeed. The thought that it might have been chance is close to ridiculous. Crediting the origins of science to chance[132] would be like assuming that a telephone or a motorcar appeared without human intervention simply by chance.

Given all this evidence for God, one may ask, why do western nations contain so many atheists?[133] We have already looked at fundamental errors currently being made by scholars in their (ab)use of the category religion. I suggest that they are making parallel errors in their (mis)understanding of God. If he is first defined sufficiently narrowly it could be possible to provide evidence against his existence. Saying: "If god exists then he must be in the bath. We can't see him in the bath therefore he does not exist" is the kind of wildly misguided thinking that these days goes on. One suspects that amongst other things it has been inspired by certain western and especially Protestant forms of Christianity. Some Protestant Christians have attempted to authoritatively over-narrowly define who or what God is. Those who challenge what they say appear to be disproving God's existence, when what they are actually disproving or contradicting is the over-narrow hermeneutics on which the particular Protestants are building. For example, Dawkins in his recent book on magic mocks the notion that "supernatural magic" can be

---

[132] In the western sense of the word chance, such as "way things happen of themselves" or "absence of design or discoverable cause" (Concise Oxford Dictionary 1982).

[133] Some people's claims to being atheists are suspect, according to Johnson (Thomas K. Johnson, e-mail message to author, May 5, 2015).

"real."[134] Both categories, supernatural and real, are not in my understanding biblical concepts, but they may be concepts used in contemporary times in an attempt to convince secularists to believe in God. As explained above, such arguments are fallacious not because of the absence of God, but because of the artificiality of the categories that they use. (The "culprit," we could say again, is Christianity. It is Christianity that proves incredibly innovative in today's world.) In recent modern use, the term atheism tends to be used to describe the negation of falsely narrow and peculiarly Christian articulations of God. Frankly, most Christian believers have moved on from these anyway, a fact that many atheists have not realized. When they do realize this it can rather disgruntle them. (See chapter 6.)

Until the above adjustments have been made to extant discourse, scholarship about religion, about life, about society, about hope, and about most other things, can be extremely nonsensical. The mind boggles to cite examples. These days some (if not many) scholars *deny* adherence to Christianity, while not only actually implicitly adhering to Christian principles, but also presupposing that Muslims, animists, Hindus and so on are all profoundly "Christian" (as argued above). I hope that by this point our understanding of life has been broadened. In a sense I want to say—I hope we have learned that religion is actually essential to life. But that would be saying we have discovered above, that Christianity is essential to life. The latter is not true in every sense, because there are some people who live but who are not Christians, e.g., Hindus in traditional India. So then what are Hindus and how are they to be best understood? Perhaps the furthest we can safely go is to say that many of them appear to be people who do not yet know Christ.

Once we have drawn the conclusion that a system that brings value (i.e., religion) to people is essential for normal human existence, then that raises the question of which system to choose? That is to say—which way of life is "best"? Of course, there is no other way to determine the answer to this question than through theology. It is a question that in the end only God can answer. Without God's intervention, people can only make guesses. Humans must answer such a question according to their understanding of who God is. People are implicitly answering this question through the choices that they make in life. Hence, of course, people are, whether they claim to be "religious" or not, constantly making implicitly theological choices.

---

[134] Dawkins, *Magic of Reality*, 19.

7. Finding a Foundation for Life

Theological choices made by people are not usually "free" choices. People are brought up on the basis of implicit understandings that arise from choices made by previous generations. For example, if you are brought up as a Muslim, generally you have little choice but to stay a Muslim, unless you are prepared to accept a major re-orientation to your way of life, which may include being rejected by your biological family or being killed. This is not a free open world of free choices. But neither is it free of personal responsibility. On the contrary, individuals in the system can make *some* choices. They need to make those choices wisely. An enormous way in which such choices have been made and are being made is very evident in many parts of sub-Saharan Africa. Vast numbers of sub-Saharan people have become adherents to Christianity. Others have become adherents of Islam. Although there may be different degrees of coercion involved, especially in the case of Islam,[135] there have been and there are also many individual choices. At the very least we can say that *many African people have made choices that seem to limit the jurisdiction of their departed ancestors.* They prefer the rule of God to the rule of spirits. According to widespread terminology, in many African languages the name for "ancestral spirit" is translated into English as devil or Satan. (See for example Douglas.[136]) Many African people have clearly demonstrated, through their choice to become Christians, that they prefer the rule of God to the rule of the devil.

I want at this point to go back to some language issues. The failure to understand language has, I suggest, been a basic reason for a lot of the confusion that has resulted in the contemporary prominence of secularist belief. Bergen, writing as recently as 2012, is just one example of a scholar who seems to be very reluctant to fully acknowledge either the power of language in determining understanding, or the vulnerability of language understanding to the culture of the people who use it. Bergen studies ways in which the mind makes meaning.[137] He finds that people make meaning through a process of embodied simulation. That is to say, that human thoughts seem not to be abstract pieces of mentalese. ("A hypothetical language in which concepts and propositions are represent-

---

[135] I do not here have the space to make a detailed investigation of the use of coercion in the interests of conversion into Christianity, Islam, or other ontologies (religions). I think though I can safely say that Islam's means of conversion has been particularly strongly rooted in coercion, whereas Christianity's much less so.
[136] Douglas, *Sorcery Accusations*, 178.
[137] Bergen, *Louder Than Words*.

ed in the mind without words.")[138] Instead, they are always (as far as Bergen could extend his research) connected to embodied life. Hence he suggests that people's thoughts cannot be separated from their cultures. At the same time he denies the ability of cultural practices to change word meaning: "the idea that cultural practices can change the individual meaning of a word so radically is still a hypothesis," he tells us.[139] As far as Bergen is concerned, there is no empirical evidence for this.[140] Later Bergen acknowledges that "the people who speak different languages as part of belonging to different cultures understand the same language about the same events differently."[141] His reluctance to acknowledge the major impact of people's cultures on their understanding of language could be arising from two sources. One, many dominant western scholars, especially Americans and Brits, are monolingual and so have a poor grasp of translation issues. Two, acknowledging the impact of culture on understanding undermines both some of the ambitions of globally-oriented universities, and of people of different cultures who have adopted European languages on the basis that they can understand them. Western academics taking the world by storm in the globalization of education may not appreciate being told that what they are endeavoring is impossible to do.

Western academia seems to be reluctant to realize what ought to be obvious regarding language. That is the sheer difficulties involved in intercultural communication, especially where the same language is used cross-culturally. I have addressed this issue in numerous other places, for example see Harries.[142] This failure to perceive difficulties helps to explain why many western scholars, who tend to be dominant in global scholarship, have failed to perceive some of the implications for "religion" of globalization that we are looking at in this text.

Language is not what it is sometimes made out to be. It can be helpful to enlighten us. It can also mislead us. It can inform us. It can conceal information. It can certainly distort and control facts. Certainly interculturally—relying on a language such as English to inform us of what is going on in other cultures is fraught. It would seem that structures built outside of the West with global languages as their foundation may not be all that they appear. "Structures" built in Africa would certainly be a case

---

[138] http://www.thefreedictionary.com/mentalese
[139] Bergen, *Louder Than Words*, 183.
[140] Ibid.
[141] Ibid., 187.
[142] Harries, *Contribution of the Use*.

7. Finding a Foundation for Life

in point. Given this perspective on language in addition to everything else that has been said above, it may appear that "much undermining has been undermined"; more on that below. We could here make reference to Matthew 7:24-27, and say that secularism has been endeavoring to build its house on sand:

> Therefore everyone who hears these words of mine and puts them into practice is like a wise man who built his house on the rock. The rain came down, the streams rose, and the winds blew and beat against that house; yet it did not fall, because it had its foundation on the rock. But everyone who hears these words of mine and does not put them into practice is like a foolish man who built his house on sand. The rain came down, the streams rose, and the winds blew and beat against that house, and it fell with a great crash. (NIV)

8. Undermining Has Been Undermined

I once read an anthropologist's description of missionary work in East Africa. He clearly thought he knew much better than did the missionaries on the station that he studied. The missionaries seemed to be blundering and incompetent. They were naive, the anthropologist was well informed. They were under qualified for their task whereas their critic was highly educated. The missionaries were on all accounts destroying people's culture, which the anthropologist carefully avoided doing. So at least was the gist of the account.[143] A closer look reveals that many anthropologists have depended on missionaries in various ways. They used the missionary infrastructure to get where they wanted to go. Insights from missionaries got them launched into their studies and gave them the basic understanding they needed to start out with.[144] While missionaries almost invariably advocated high moral standards for local people, anthropologists were less intent on doing so. Anthropologists committed at most a year or two on the field—a foundation enabling them to have a career in academia, whereas missionaries gave their lives—frequently twenty, thirty or even forty years of service. There is little doubt today that it is places where missionaries, for all their foibles, have been used by God to plant Christianity that are the most open for anthropological inquiry. Many Islamized regions of Africa, for example, are much less accessible to anthropologists and other Westerners than are Christianized parts of the continent. Do anthropologists and the secularists who back them need to offer Christian missionaries a big apology?

Arguments that were in recent decades and centuries used to undermine the relevance of missionary activity in Africa seem to have themselves been undermined. Anthropologists such as Beidelman (above) considered themselves to have had a foundation from which to evaluate and criticize missionary activity. It has since been realized that the said foundation is not what it appeared. At the same time we have to admit even now, that while foundationalism has been undermined, the momentum gained during the heydays of foundationalists' faith is still very much with us. The outcomes of the now undermined means of undermining the Christian faith have for many become now we have to say by faith (as there is no longer any other basis for believing what they believe) the

---

[143] Beidelman, *Colonial Evangelism*.
[144] Harries and Maxwell, *Introduction*, 20.

foundation of their way(s) of life. The undermined underminings are not only "out there" to be looked at rather as one might consider a paradigm or intellectual tradition. Rather, they have been closely incorporated into ways of life in the West, indeed into the very languages used by the West. English, as used in the West, is certainly a case in point of an example of a language that is shot-through with presuppositions that can no longer be said (following arguments that we have made above) to be firmly grounded in "reality."

Some may ask, how can a language carry ways of life? That is—how can a language be "shot-through" with presuppositions? Contrary to those who hold conduit theories of language and consider languages like a vehicle that carry meanings, I am not claiming that languages themselves carry philosophies, ideologies or other such content.[145] I do suggest however that for their correct functioning, languages do presuppose a great deal. In this sense European languages are like a Trojan horse, but a Trojan horse that never overtly reveals its contents to those to whom it is delivered. Because languages are used by people to reflect and express realities that they live, certain language uses tally with certain ways of life. This means that transferring a language from one cultural context to another can render that language ineffective. In other words, as language meanings arise from the ways in which a language is used,[146] the same language in a different context should either be used differently, or at very least will be used on the basis of different word meanings. When for example English is used in Africa, the same language is used in a different context. Yet the international community expects it to be used in the same way as in the West, using the same dictionaries. Here we have a problem.

I can illustrate the above at this point with examples. I take examples of different sports in my article published in 2011.[147] I now want to draw on what has already been mentioned above in this text. I have suggested that the global use of the term religion to describe the ways of life of non-Christians is in some ways illegitimate. It is loaded with endless false presuppositions, based on Christianity, that are supposedly extant amongst non-Christian peoples around the world. Yet the existence of the particular category religion is central to a great deal of western thinking. For example, if there is no longer a category of religion that can be kept aside

---

[145] For a critique of conduit theories of language see Mojola and Wendland, *Scripture Translation*, 7.
[146] Harries, *Pragmatic Theory*, 29.
[147] Harries, *Is It Post-Modern*.

8. Undermining Has Been Undermined

and leave rationality intact to function "by itself," then rationality is no longer (in that sense) rational. We can go further in our exploration into language. Despite those who have pointed to the contrary, there are still people who believe that there are facts that cannot be disputed, that are absolute, and that can therefore legitimately be used as foundations for further thinking. We should by now have realized from this text that selection amongst facts being in many ways arbitrary (if one discounts the intervention of a divine agent) renders facts into the outcome of choices. As a result, "facts" cannot legitimately be considered to be a part of an objective foundation for life.

Let us consider further examples: the modern world has chosen to try to undermine differences between the male and female genders. As a result, women get "rights" to freedom. In the process however, children lose their "rights" to having mothers. While the sheer biological reality of mothers bearing children is acknowledged, any necessity of having a woman involved in the ongoing role of parenthood can be denied.[148] If we turn to love—it appears that the West presupposes a kind of universalism in the possession of what we could term *agape* love.[149] Western people themselves are known for their having a kind of unconditional-compassion. This has formed the foundation for thinking about international and intercultural aid. Are Westerners right to presuppose that other people have the same understanding of love? If they do not have it, yet western English presupposes it, then they cannot be considered to be equally equipped with Westerners to use English.[150] Could it be that it has arisen from centuries-long impact of Christianity? The West holding such a quality deeply (i.e., deeply valuing *agape* love) yet denying its origins, contributes to the difficulty involved in any suggestion that such a quality could be absent for other non-western people. To suggest as much brings one up against another monster elephant in the room: racism. Anti-racist strategies in the West conceal differences that Christianization

---

[148] For example, it is legally permissible in the UK for a homosexual couple to adopt and rear children (http://www.pinkparents.org.uk/same-sex-adoption-in-the-uk.html).

[149] *Agape* comes from the Greek and is often used to refer to "selfless love."

[150] If English is culturally loaded, as this implies, then it cannot be true that English can be taught equally well by non-native as by native speakers. If this is the case, then the use of English as a kind of global language is heavily loaded in favor of empowering native English users and confusing non-native English users. If these two groups are considered to be using one and not two Englishes, contemporary efforts at forcing two Englishes into one is a source of a lot of contemporary failures in understanding.

brings to non-western communities.[151] The need for their being Christianized thus having been concealed adds fuel to arguments regarding the non-necessity of Christianity, and so it goes on.

It can seem as if the West, having blundered upon means of generating enormous wealth (arising, as I have indicated above, in many ways from Christianity), that this wealth has gone to its head. Having begun with dependence on God, and crediting the Holy Spirit with gifts even in the realms of medicine, technology etc., they have moved to a misguided pride in an objective ability that is in actuality subjectively dependent on divine intervention. The cruelty of this position should not be missed. It may not have any murderous intent. But it may nevertheless have a death-causing outcome. Just by way of example—enormous subsidy of various kinds that comes with western (English language, British/American-based) education makes this education (expressed in European languages) the default option of choice of millions and millions of people in Africa. When a system becomes so hegemonic, then alternatives are suppressed and have no chance of developing. For example—in numerous African countries it is virtually if not absolutely impossible to engage in education with any formality other than through the medium of English. At the same time, as mentioned above, use of English in Africa is full of foibles. "Forcing" (in effect) African people to use foibled-English in education, in preference to their own languages that they understand, is forcing African people to use extremely faulty tools. (Unlike native English speakers, African people who appropriate English are not *au fait* with its many cultural and philosophical quirks.) As a result, Africa does not prosper and/or develop without enormous dependency on the West. Aid and foreign dependency become the substitute for indigenously-driven development. Such aid easily misses many of the masses: distribution of aid is usually not easy. Those who do not get the aid die. Such kind of "killing" that arises from rendering people incompetent, and then making them dependent on unreliable aid may not be recognized as a crime in international law (or most national laws for that matter), but results in mass death nevertheless.[152]

---

[151] Harries, *Anti-Racist Strategies*.
[152] Green points to a parallel to the "killing" that I am suggesting is going on here. Green suggests that promotion of certain kinds of behavior that are supposedly oriented to alleviating the AIDS crisis by the West have recently been aggravating it. In brief, advocating so-called prophylactics such as condoms has, according to Green, caused millions of deaths that could have been avoided if faithfulness to one partner in marriage had instead been promoted. (Green, *Broken Promises*.)

8. Undermining Has Been Undermined

The above paragraph states a clear urgency to our task. I believe that urgency to be very real. The system as it stands is criss-crossed by serious "fatal" fault-lines. That is not to say that what we need is revolution. It is not to say that we need a forceful overthrowing of the global status quo. The overthrowing of one corrupt and corrupting system can all too easily be followed by the development of another. I would prefer to suggest a different course of action. I have gone into this in more detail in a paper currently in press, in which I advocate for *champions*.[153] These champions must really be Christians because the godly task required of them is one that only Christians are likely to be desiring to perform. It is not a task that requires us first to wait for a build-up of momentum that critiques the status quo or for conditions to be right. It is a task that requires someone to make sacrifices in Christian service. I believe that there is in our age of globalization an urgent need for Westerners who are prepared to cross intercultural divides; those who are ready to follow Christ's commands to offer themselves as living sacrifices (Rom 12:2) in the interests of the work of the Gospel of Christ. It seems incredible if not "criminal" to me at times that this is not happening more. We hear stories of in bygone centuries scores of Christian missionaries being dead within a few years of reaching Africa.[154] That did not deter more from coming. In our own day travel and life in foreign parts has been made easier and easier. Even in Africa, early death is relatively unlikely, but despite all this very few if any contemporary western Christians give themselves to overseas service, unless they are there to represent foreign money and to spread the use of European languages.[155]

I ought at this stage to mention the "romantic." A popular European notion has been that non-western people, uncluttered as they are with trappings of wealth and depressing aspects of sophistication, are living romantic ideal lives. Majorly contributing to this notion, I suggest, was the confusion between sin and taboo mentioned in chapter 6. Other western myths have contributed to such naive beliefs. The reality speaks rather differently. In Africa as elsewhere, if people were living as freely and joyously as romantic notions would have us believe, then presumably they would be endeavoring to prevent inroads of the Gospel of Christ into

---

[153] Harries, *Anti-Racist Strategies*.
[154] http://www.byfaith.co.uk/paul20091.htm
[155] Almost all service by western missionaries in Africa today is dependent on an ongoing flow of charitable funds from the West and/or on the ongoing use of European languages. This combination of circumstances should be a serious cause of concern.

their communities. I do not see such happening in Africa. On the contrary, African folk (unless they are already Islamic) often seem to be the keenest Christians as well as the most enthusiastic appropriators of western ways of life. In Africa the Christian church grows in leaps and bounds.[156] Western educational systems are loved. Western languages are preferred. Western clothes are worn. Mobile phones and computers have become all the rage even for "poor" African communities—as soon as they can be afforded. The romantic idea of the "noble savage" seems to be a misguided western invention.[157]

Remove the romantic noble savage from view, and a lot of associated baggage disappears with him. Let us consider Africa's interest in Christianity. It should not, according to secularists and modernists who like to perpetuate romantic myths, be there. I am not saying that all Christian missionaries are constantly on cloud nine enjoying great success in their evangelistic endeavors. The church has not turned out just as the missionaries wanted it to. Of course there are problems. There is too much dependency and prosperity gospel. Yet the church is very much there in many parts of Africa. Really, it seems to be very much there wherever Islam does not dominate. This was not and is not really to be expected by modernists. African people are voting with their feet for a holistic development. That is to say, they are seeing a key or primary role for the spiritual or religious in their pursuance of the material.

---

[156] Jenkins, *Next Christendom*, 39.
[157] Pinker, *Blank Slate*, 26.

9. Brave New World of One "Religion"

I would like to come towards a close to this text by considering what the world would look like if a change in the way language is used were to be made, so that we were left with only one "religion." The "religion" that has been integral to the development of the West has clearly been Christianity, and one could say western Christianity. English has developed and grown in the same western world, so that when it uses the term "religion" it is very much Christianity that it implicitly refers to. The same western world is the origin and source of much of the technological thinking that has brought so many changes to contemporary peoples. This has arisen in the same Christian context. The modern system of secular education has grown in a Christian context, and fanned out to the rest of the world from there.

Christianity at one time contrasted itself much more strongly to "other religions" than it sometimes does now. It saw itself as purveying truth in a world where there was much error. This position of declared presumed superiority has largely been taken over by that offshoot from Christian belief often known as secularism. Secularism has at the same time become the adversary against which western Christians tend to pitch themselves. We could say that it is the twentieth and twenty-first century heresy. Secularism's hegemonic claims are enormous. It has attempted and is attempting to relegate all "religions" to a secondary status, and to take singular global control of a large chunk of human life and values. Its success so far in doing has been remarkable. So-called secular states, secular governments, secular education, secular economies, secular armies etc. are much referred to around the world.

Perhaps, I suggest in this text, the ascendancy of secularism is not quite what it appears to be. Perhaps adherence to secularism around the world is only skin deep. Africa certainly seems to be a case in point. Activities that could really only be termed religious abound in supposedly secular and secularizing African communities.[158] Children follow school curricula which appear to be rooted in secularism, while their families are endlessly embroiled in religiously rooted disputes, rituals, and activities, never mind hopes and fears. Perhaps global secularism is not so

---

[158] South Africa claims to be a secular state, yet over 90% of its people claim to be highly religious, according to Burchardt. (http://www.multiple-secularities.de/project_sa_en.html accessed August 28, 2014)

global at all. Perhaps—its reach extends only as far as the immediate influence of the Christian West that invented it. Evidence to this effect actually abounds. The only place people seem to have abandoned their temples, prayers, rituals and devotions is in parts of the West itself. People in other parts of the world adopt the label secularism because of its power, not because they are at all convinced by its ideologies as understood in the West.

This is where we should be perceiving again the problem we identified above with the label "religion." The label comes from the West (English comes from the West). It was originally used to refer to Christianity. It describes something that because it is a compliment to secularism is supposed to be non-hegemonic over people's lives. The term "religion" is in the contemporary West used in such a way as to presume that there is something in life that is other than religion or not religious. It presumes that there are two things: the secular and the religious. But what if, for other people around the world who are not Westerners, there are no such two distinct categories? What if, as appears to be the case in many parts of Africa, Muslim lands, Hindu lands, etc., secularism quickly loses its pure imported nature? Once secularism becomes a part of a people's way of life "as any other," then how can it be seen as being non-religious or distinct from religion? This means that in those lands, neither secularism nor religion as defined in the West can exist. Looking at it this way, it can easily appear that there is only one "religion." That is—there is only one way of life that allows the "secular" to thrive alongside its own practices. That is (western) Christianity. In this sense then—the only "real" religion is Christianity or western Christianity or parts of western Christianity from which secularism has arisen.[159]

The West has been and seems to continue to be desperate to prove that the above is not the case. That is to say—secularists scour the world seeking verification for their beliefs. When they do so using English, then they find what they are looking for, although they are not always realizing that it is their own presuppositions that they are reading back into

---

[159] Although I will continue to use the term Christian generically, there is of course a great deal of variety within Christianity. The division between eastern and western Christianity is especially critical for our discussion. Secularism and the West as we know it today after all arose from the western church and not from the eastern church, as pointed out by Huntington (*Clash of Civilisations*, 158). Huntington looks especially at the division of the Roman Empire in the fourth century, and the creation of the Holy Roman Empire in the tenth century.

9. Brave New World of One "Religion"

other people's statements.[160] Fortunately or unfortunately, the strength of secularism is also its weakness. The strength that I refer to here is money. Secularism is to do with material things, money included. It seeks and has sought to isolate the material from the spiritual, so that the material can be developed, enlarged, empowered and given a "non-religious" identity. Promoting an ideology with the money to back it unfortunately has drawbacks; particularly in many non-western cultures where a "yes" response is default, whereas a "no" response is avoided if at all possible. This applies particularly to poorer parts of the world, which is much of the non-western world.[161] When heavily subsidized secular education and thought are proposed to poor people, the answer can often be "yes, give me the money." To verify the genuineness of secularism, one would have to see non-Westerners promote it and advocate it in ways that weren't financially lucrative. Is that really happening? It would seem not. In short; if secularism only spreads on the back of money, then how does one know that money is not simply buying apparent adherence to what is not being understood?

To use different terminology—it would appear that Christianity is not only *the* dualistic religion par excellence. It is also the only dualistic "religion." That is, it is (or parts of it are) the only "religion" that thrives while happy to allow secularism to prosper alongside it. Huntington seems to confirm this: "the separation . . . between church and state that typify Western civilisation have existed in no other civilisation."[162] The close link between secularism and Christianity is evident even in more recent times. Taking the UK as example, we can see that it can be easy for Christian churches to follow secular trends. The rise of feminism has resulted in the Anglican Church accepting female bishops.[163] According to a BBC report, "with the decision, the Church is acknowledging the importance secular society places on equality, signalling that it wants to end its isolation from the lives of the people it serves."[164] Recently a turn-

---

[160] A senior African church leader once told me as we sat in Nairobi that more and more Kenyan people were rejecting the church in favour of "secularism." As our conversation continued, I came to realize that his use of the term secularism included allegiance to "traditional religions."
[161] This is only partly true. Parts of the non-western world have become very wealthy.
[162] Huntington, *Clash of Civilisations*, 70.
[163] http://www.bbc.com/news/uk-28300618
[164] http://www.bbc.com/news/uk-28300618 Even if the church might deny that it is "following secular trends," there is clearly a popular view that this is what it is doing.

about in secular government position that has declared homosexuality legal and given homosexuals legal rights has resulted in many churches following suit, and adjusting their theologies as a result. The western church has grown accustomed to operating under a co-operative secular system. It is used to filling the gaps that secularism leaves. It expects the secular system also to pay attention to it. When secularism oversteps its mark, overtakes the church, and impinges on the territory of the church, the church is inclined to fall in line. Other supposed "religions" seem to be less passive in the face of secularism.[165]

My main point here though is to say that if religions are those parts of human existence that fall outside of the category of secularism, and if it is only western Christianity that does this, then this means that the other "religions" are not religions at all. Their being termed religions is therefore a category error; the practice of calling them "religions" is illegitimate.

The western world has long been engaging in an implicit transfer of pre-suppositional assumptions to where they do not belong. The transfer is from Christianity to other people's ways-of-life around the world. Westerners who have observed things in other parts of the world that seem to parallel the Christianity they are used to at home, have assumed that they must therefore fall in the same category. They have assumed that the category is distinct from "the secular," that it resembles Christianity, and they have given that category the label *religion*. The study of other "religions," on account of the fact that they are religions, has included an implicit carry-over of content from Christianity. It has assumed a legitimacy in comparison between "other religions" and Christianity. It has assumed that they are somehow equivalents, that they can be substituted for one another. This has been and continues to be the framing for endless debates. As shared by Lakoff: framing is critical![166]

The above assumption of equivalence has been and is largely untrue. Let's say at least that it has been as much illegitimate as it has been legitimate. It has been and it continues to be grossly misleading. As pointed out above—this misleadingness has not been neutral. It marks an enormous blind spot in western academia. Implicit and explicit comparison between "other religions" and Christianity has been a massive and con-

---

[165] See for example http://islam.about.com/od/islamsays/a/homosexuality.htm on the side of Islam and http://www.religionfacts.com/homosexuality/comparison_chart.htm that compares different ways-of-life's responses to issues of homosexuality.
[166] https://www.youtube.com/watch?v=5f9R9MtkpqM

9. Brave New World of One "Religion" 97

stant source of mostly unperceived bias. It would almost certainly not be difficult to amass evidence for ways in which such bias has *denied* many non-western people from benefiting from the fruits that arise from faith in Christ. In other words: this biased way of looking at Christianity has resulted in some people even from the West turning "against" Christianity in favor of "other religions."

It is important to point to a prerogative on the side of the West to bringing the task of secularization to its natural fruition. The West and the so-called international community[167] use massive amounts of resources in the interests of promoting secularism around the world.[168] They have all too often been silent on the other half of the deal. That other half is Christianity. Secularism cannot take true local root if the accompanying belief system does not and cannot accommodate it. Instead, what can result from the spread of secularism is a spreading of dependence on the West[169]—something that we are increasingly seeing in the globalizing world. Denying people a knowledge of Christ while promoting secularism is advocating half-knowledge. It produces an unstable ideology that thrives on dependency. The promotion of secularism devoid of its Christian background is of dubious benefit. Such promotion could even be considered to be criminal.[170]

It should be evident to my reader that extending the label of "religion" beyond the boundaries of Christianity has, in addition to the concerns mentioned above, given a misleading impression of godliness to that which is heathen. It has seriously blurred boundaries. Amongst the outcomes of this has been a cooling of Christian missionary zeal. Many Christians in the West have been confused by their "secular governments'" involvement in non-secular affairs (i.e., involvement outside of

---

[167] The "international community" is guided by various global bodies, whose origins are in notions of international law that themselves originate in Christianity. The primary languages and worldviews presupposed by the same global bodies are western, i.e., are those that have emerged in the course of the history of the western church.
[168] I include, for example, funding for development in Africa to fall largely under this category.
[169] In some senses a spreading of dependency on Christianity.
[170] I am not here advocating that global bodies that are promoting secularism, such as the UN or World Bank should necessarily begin preaching the Gospel of Christ. The involvement of government-level organizations in promoting the church may be of dubious advantage. This does not however negate the nature of the issue that I am pointing to above. I use the term "criminal" in the generic sense of being offensive to humane morality.

the West, because as mentioned above there is no "secularism" outside of the West). In some so-called "Christian countries" overt belief has gone into decline. The confusion at home has extended to confusion abroad. Observing others through Christian-tinted spectacles can result in the false impression that they are very Christian. The tendency to do this seems to be all around us. For example, although the activities of Muslim extremism are increasingly recognized, the source of the extremism is at the same time officially denied. Muslims, being "religious," should according to dominant secular thinking, actually of course behave like Christians after all (because they are "religious"). When they do not so behave, then contemporary "secular" people can be shocked.

It is indeed incredible that a people can be so misled by miscategorizations in their own languages. Correction in this area is desperately needed for the sake of the future of the globe. The culprit that I have overtly pointed to here is the term religion. This is in contemporary usage a grossly misleading word. I hope that this text might get a readership that have the power to right some of the basic wrongs mentioned herein.

Bibliography

Alexander, Neville. "English Unassailable But Unattainable: The Dilemma of Language Policy in South African Education." Paper presented at the Biennial Conference of the International Federation for the Teaching of English, University of Warwick, England, UK, July 7–10, 1999. Accessed August 28, 2008. http://eric.ed.gov/ERICWebPortal/recordDetail?accno=ED444151

Anderson, Allan. *African Reformation: African Initiated Christianity in the 20th Century.* Africa World Press, 2001.

Anthony, Marcus. "A Genealogy of the Western Rationalist Hegemony." Article 25, *Journal of Futures Studies* May 2006, 25–38.

Asad, Talal. "The Construction of Religion as an Anthropological Category." In *A Reader in the Anthropology of Religion*, edited by Michael Lambeck, 115–32. Oxford: Blackwell Publishing, 2002.

———. "Responding to Gil Anidjar." *Interventions: International Journal of Post-Colonial Studies* 11, no.3 (2009) 394–99.

Beckwith, Francis J. "Faith, Reason, and Secular Hegemony." *The Catholic Thing.* April 13, 2012. Accessed August 28, 2014. http://www.thecatholicthing.org/columns/2012/faith-reason-and-secular-hegemony.html

Beidelman, T. O. *Colonial Evangelism: A Socio-Historical Study of an East African Mission at the Grassroots.* Bloomington: Indiana University Press, 1982.

Bergen, Benjamin K. *Louder Than Words: The New Science of How the Mind Makes Meaning.* New York: Basic Books, 2012.

Bronkema, David. "Flying Blind? Christian NGOs and Political Economy." In *Christian Mission and Economic Systems: A Critical Survey of the Cultural and Religious Dimensions of Economies*, edited by John Cheong and Eloise Meneses, 144–68. Pasadena: William Carey Library, 2015.

Brutt-Griffler, Janina. *World English: A Study of Its Development.* Bristol: Multilingual Matters. 2002.

Calhoun, Craig et al. "Introduction." In *Rethinking Secularism,* edited by Craig Calhoun et al., 3–30. Oxford: Oxford University Press, 2011.

Cannell, Fennella. "The Christianity of Anthropology." *Journal of the Royal Anthropological Institute* 11 (2005) 335–56.

———, ed. *The Anthropology of Christianity.* Durham, NC: Duke University Press, 2006.

Chang, Ha-Joon. *Kicking Away the Ladder: Development Strategy in Historical Perspective.* London: Anthem Press, 2002.

Dawkins, Richard. *The Magic of Reality: How We Know What's Really True.* London: Free Press, 2012.

———. *An Appetite for Wonder: The Making of a Scientist.* New York: Ecco, 2014.

Djité, Paulin G. *The Sociolinguistics of Development in Africa.* Clevedon: Multilingual Matters, 2008.

Douglas, Mary. *Purity and Danger: An Analysis of the Concepts of Pollution and Taboo.* London: Routledge & Kegan Paul, 1966.

———. "Sorcery Accusations Unleashed: The Lele Revisited, 1987." *Africa: Journal of the International African Institute* 69 (1999) 177–93. Accessed October 21, 2005. http://links.jstor.org/sici=0001-9720%281999%2969%3A2%3c177%3asautlr%3E2.0.co%3b2-V

Frazer, James George. *Folklore in the Old Testament.* New York: Macmillan, 1923.

Green, Edward C. *Broken Promises: How the AIDS Establishment Has Betrayed the Developing World.* Sausalito, CA: Poli Point Press LLC, 2011. Kindle edition.

Harries, Jim. "Pragmatic Theory Applied to Christian Mission in Africa: With Special Reference to Luo Responses to 'Bad' in Gem, Kenya."

PhD Thesis, University of Birmingham, 2007. Accessed January 2, 2010. http://etheses.bham.ac.uk/15/

———. "International Development Without Money? Some Theological Reflections." In *The Goal of International Development: God's Will on Earth, as It Is in Heaven*, edited by Beth Snodderly, 145–56. Pasadena: WCIU Press, 2009.

———, 2011a. "The Immorality of Aid to the 'Third World' (Africa)." In *Vulnerable Mission; Insights into Christian Mission to Africa From a Position of Vulnerability*, 23–40. Pasadena: William Carey Library, 2011.

———, 2011b. "The Magical Worldview in the African Church: What Is Going On?" In *Vulnerable Mission; Insights into Christian Mission to Africa From a Position of Vulnerability*, 203–24. Pasadena: William Carey Library, 2011.

———, 2011c. "'Is it Post-Modern, or is it just the Real Thing?' Challenging Inter-cultural Mission—a Parable." *Global Missiology* 3, no. 8 (2011). (http://ojs.globalmissiology.org/index.php/english/article/view/585)

———, 2012a. "The Contribution of the Use of English in Africa to Dependency in Mission and Development." *Exchange, Journal of Missiological and Ecumenical Research* 41, no.3 (2012) 279–94.

———, 2012b. "Witchcraft, Envy, Development, and Christian Mission in Africa." *Missiology: An International Review* 40, no.2 (2012) 129–39.

———. "Anti-Racist Strategies in the West Perpetuate Global Poverty: A Critique from Africa." *Cultural Encounters: A Journal for the Theology of Culture* 10, no.2 (2014).

———. "Sin v. Taboo Compatibility in Africa and the West: Implications for Inter-Cultural Mission, Church, and Majority World Development." *Evangelical Review of Theology* 39, no.2 (2015) 157–169.

———. *Secularism and Africa: In the Light of the Intercultural Christ*. Oregon: Wipf & Stock, 2015.

Harries, Patrick, and David Maxwell. "Introduction." In *The Spiritual in the Secular: Missionaries and Knowledge about Africa (Studies in the History of*

Christian Missions), edited by Patrick Harries and David Maxwell, 1–29. Michigan: Wm. B. Eerdmans Publishing Company, 2012.

Hiebert, Paul. *Missiological Implications of Epistemological Shifts: Affirming Truth in a Modern/Postmodern World.* Harrisburg: Trinity Press International, 1999.

Hoehler-Fatton, Cynthia. *Women of Fire and Spirit: History, Faith and Gender in Roho Religion in Western Kenya.* Oxford: Oxford University Press, 1996.

———. "Founders and Foundresses: Revising the History of a Kenyan Independent Church." *Religion* 28, no.4 (1998) 393–404.

Holden, Lynn. "Taboos: Structure and Rebellion." *Monograph Series No. 41, The Institute for Cultural Research.* University of Edinburgh, 2001. Accessed August 9, 2014. http://www.i-c-r.org.uk/publications/monographarchive/Monograph41.pdf

Huntington, Samuel P. *The Clash of Civilizations: And the Remaking of World Order.* London: Simon and Schuster, 2002.

Jamieson, Robert et al. *A Commentary, Critical, Practical, and Explanatory on the Old and New Testament,* 1882. Accessed August 19, 2014. http://www.sacred-texts.com/bib/cmt/jfb/deu022.htm

Jenkins, Philip. *The Next Christendom: The Coming of Global Christianity.* Oxford: Oxford University Press, 2002.

Johnson, Thomas K. *The First Step in Missions Training: How Our Neighbours Are Wrestling With God's General Revelation.* Bonn: Verlag fuer Kultur und Wissenschaft, 2014.

Kuhn, T. S. *The Structure of Scientific Revolutions.* 2nd ed. Chicago: University of Chicago Press, 1970.

Lado, Ludovic. "The Roman Catholic Church and African Religions: A Problematic Encounter." *The Way* 45, no.3 (2006) 7–21.

Lakoff, George, and Mark Johnson. *Philosophy in the Flesh: The Embodied Mind and Its Challenge to Western Thought.* New York: Basic Books, 1999.

Larner, Christina. *Witchcraft and Religion: The Politics of Popular Belief.* Oxford: Basil Blackwell, 1984.

Larsen, Timothy. *The Slain God: Anthropologists and the Christian Faith.* Oxford: Oxford University Press, 2014.

Maranz, David. *African Friends and Money Matters: Observations from Africa.* Dallas: SIL International, 2001.

Marsden, George M. *The Outrageous Idea of Christian Scholarship.* Oxford: Oxford University Press, 1997.

Mohr, Richard. "The Christian Origins of Secularism and the Rule of Law." In *Law and Religion in Public Life: The Contemporary Debate*, edited by Nadirsyah Hosen and Richard Mohr, 34-51. Abingdon: Routledge, 2011.

Mojola, Aloo Osotsi, and Ernst Wendland. "Scripture Translation in the Era of Translation Studies." In *Bible Translation: Frames of Reference*, edited by Timothy Wilt, 1-25. Manchester: St Jerome Publishing, 2003.

Mutua, Makau. *Human Rights: A Political and Cultural Critique* (Pennsylvania Studies in Human Rights). Pennsylvania: University of Pennsylvania Press, 2008.

NEH Summer Seminar 2004. "The Seven Deadly Sins as Cultural Constructions in the Middle Ages." Accessed August 9, 2014. http://www.trinity.edu/rnewhaus/outline.html

Ogot, Bethwell A. "Reverend Alfayo Odongo Mango 1870-1934." In *Reintroducing Man into the African World: Selected Essays 1961-1980*, 109-31. Kisumu: Anyange Press Ltd. 1999.

Pinker, Steven. *The Blank Slate: The Modern Denial of Human Nature.* London: Penguin, 2002.

Plantinga, Alvin. "Reason and Belief in God." In *Faith and Rationality: Reason and Belief in God*, edited by A. Plantinga and N. Wolterstorff, 16-93. London: University of Notre Dame Press, 1983.

Priest, Robert J. "Cultural Anthropology, Sin, and the Missionary." In *God and Culture: Essays in Honor of Carl F. H. Henry*, edited by D. A. Carson and John Woodbridge, 85–105. Carlisle: The Paternoster Press, 1993.

———. "Missionary Positions: Christian, Modernist, Postmodernist." *Current Anthropology* 42, No.1 (2001) 29–68.

Raringo, Jacktone Keya. *Chike Jaduong e Dalane*. No publisher, no date.

Reitan, Eric. "Moving the Goalposts? The Challenge of Philosophical Engagement With the Public God Debates." *Philo* 13, no.1 (2010) 80–93.

Robbins, Joel et al. "Evangelical Conversion and the Transformation of the Self in Amazonia and Melanesia: Christianity and the Revival of Anthropological Comparison." *Comparative Studies in Society and History*, 56, no.3 (2014) 559–90.

Rozin, Paul, and Carol Nemeroff. "The Laws of Sympathetic Magic: A Psychological Analysis of Similarity and Contagion." In *Cultural Psychology: Essays on Comparative Human Development*, edited by J. Stigler et al., 205–32. Cambridge: Cambridge University Press, 1990.

Schwartz, Glenn J. *When Charity Destroys Dignity: Overcoming Unhealthy Dependency in the Christian Movement*. Milton Keynes: Author House, 2007.

Spicer, Andrew. "'Of No Church': Immigrants, Liefhebbers and Confessional Diversity in Elizabethan London, c. 1568–1581." In *Forgetting Faith?: Negotiating Confessional Conflict in Early Modern Europe*, edited by Isabel Karremann et al., 199–220. Berlin: De Gruyter, 2012.

Sundkler, B. G. M. *Bantu Prophets in South Africa*. 2nd ed. London: Oxford University Press, 1961.

Venuti, Lawrence. *The Scandals of Translation: Towards an Ethics of Difference*. London: Routledge, 1998.

Welbourn, F. B. "Towards Eliminating the Concept of Religion." Delivered to the Colloquium on the Concept of Religion. Lancaster University, December 1969.

Williams, Rowan. "Representing reality." Lecture 1 of the series: "Making Representations: Religious Faith and the Habits of Language." University of Edinburgh Gifford Lectures, November 2013. Accessed December 4, 2013. http://www.ed.ac.uk/schools-departments/humanities-soc-sci/news-events/lectures/gifford-lectures/williams-oystermouth/lecture-one

Young, Robert C. *Colonial Desire: Hybridity in Theory, Culture and Race*. London: Routledge, 1995.

Biography

Jim Harries (PhD theology, University of Birmingham) has lived and served as a missionary in Africa, initially in Zambia then more recently in East Africa, since 1988. His primary formal occupation apart from research/writing and caring for his (informally) adopted African children is Bible teaching with indigenous churches. Jim relates to the African community around him using the Luo and Swahili indigenous languages. He makes major efforts to ensure that many of his significant relationships with African people not be based on their expectation of material gain. Jim has published five books, and numerous articles related to missiology, intercultural communication, development and especially vulnerable mission. He is the chairman of the AVM (Alliance for Vulnerable Mission).

World Evangelical Alliance

World Evangelical Alliance is a global ministry working with local churches around the world to join in common concern to live and proclaim the Good News of Jesus in their communities. WEA is a network of churches in 129 nations that have each formed an evangelical alliance and over 100 international organizations joining together to give a worldwide identity, voice and platform to more than 600 million evangelical Christians. Seeking holiness, justice and renewal at every level of society – individual, family, community and culture, God is glorified and the nations of the earth are forever transformed.

Christians from ten countries met in London in 1846 for the purpose of launching, in their own words, "a new thing in church history, a definite organization for the expression of unity amongst Christian individuals belonging to different churches." This was the beginning of a vision that was fulfilled in 1951 when believers from 21 countries officially formed the World Evangelical Fellowship. Today, 150 years after the London gathering, WEA is a dynamic global structure for unity and action that embraces 600 million evangelicals in 129 countries. It is a unity based on the historic Christian faith expressed in the evangelical tradition. And it looks to the future with vision to accomplish God's purposes in discipling the nations for Jesus Christ.

Commissions:

- Theology
- Missions
- Religious Liberty
- Women's Concerns
- Youth
- Information Technology

Initiatives and Activities

- Ambassador for Human Rights
- Ambassador for Refugees
- Creation Care Task Force
- Global Generosity Network
- International Institute for Religious Freedom
- International Institute for Islamic Studies
- Leadership Institute
- Micah Challenge
- Global Human Trafficking Task Force
- Peace and Reconciliation Initiative
- UN-Team

Church Street Station
P.O. Box 3402
New York, NY 10008-3402
Phone +[1] 212 233 3046
Fax +[1] 646-957-9218
www.worldea.org

Giving Hands

GIVING HANDS GERMANY (GH) was established in 1995 and is officially recognized as a nonprofit foreign aid organization. It is an international operating charity that – up to now – has been supporting projects in about 40 countries on four continents. In particular we care for orphans and street children. Our major focus is on Africa and Central America. GIVING HANDS always mainly provides assistance for self-help and furthers human rights thinking.

The charity itself is not bound to any church, but on the spot we are cooperating with churches of all denominations. Naturally we also cooperate with other charities as well as governmental organizations to provide assistance as effective as possible under the given circumstances.

The work of GIVING HANDS GERMANY is controlled by a supervisory board. Members of this board are Manfred Feldmann, Colonel V. Doner and Kathleen McCall. Dr. Christine Schirrmacher is registered as legal manager of GIVING HANDS at the local district court. The local office and work of the charity are coordinated by Rev. Horst J. Kreie as executive manager. Dr. theol. Thomas Schirrmacher serves as a special consultant for all projects.

Thanks to our international contacts companies and organizations from many countries time and again provide containers with gifts in kind which we send to the different destinations where these goods help to satisfy elementary needs. This statutory purpose is put into practice by granting nutrition, clothing, education, construction and maintenance of training centers at home and abroad, construction of wells and operation of water treatment systems, guidance for self-help and transportation of goods and gifts to areas and countries where needy people live.

GIVING HANDS has a publishing arm under the leadership of Titus Vogt, that publishes human rights and other books in English, Spanish, Swahili and other languages.

These aims are aspired to the glory of the Lord according to the basic Christian principles put down in the Holy Bible.

Baumschulallee 3a • D-53115 Bonn • Germany
Phone: +49 / 228 / 695531 • Fax +49 / 228 / 695532
www.gebende-haende.de • info@gebende-haende.de

Martin Bucer Seminary

**Faithful to biblical truth
Cooperating with the Evangelical Alliance
Reformed**

Solid training for the Kingdom of God
- Alternative theological education
- Study while serving a church or working another job
- Enables students to remain in their own churches
- Encourages independent thinking
- Learning from the growth of the universal church.

Academic
- For the Bachelor's degree: 180 Bologna-Credits
- For the Master's degree: 120 additional Credits
- Both old and new teaching methods: All day seminars, independent study, term papers, etc.

Our Orientation:
- Complete trust in the reliability of the Bible
- Building on reformation theology
- Based on the confession of the German Evangelical Alliance
- Open for innovations in the Kingdom of God

Our Emphasis:
- The Bible
- Ethics and Basic Theology
- Missions
- The Church

Our Style:
- Innovative
- Relevant to society
- International
- Research oriented
- Interdisciplinary

Structure
- 15 study centers in 7 countries with local partners
- 5 research institutes
- President: Prof. Dr. Thomas Schirrmacher
  Vice President: Prof. Dr. Thomas K. Johnson
- Deans: Thomas Kinker, Th.D.;
  Titus Vogt, lic. theol., Carsten Friedrich, M.Th.

Missions through research
- Institute for Religious Freedom
- Institute for Islamic Studies
- Institute for Life and Family Studies
- Institute for Crisis, Dying, and Grief Counseling
- Institute for Pastoral Care

www.bucer.eu • info@bucer.eu
Berlin I Bielefeld I Bonn I Chemnitz I Hamburg I Munich I Pforzheim
Innsbruck I Istanbul I Izmir I Linz I Prague I São Paulo I Tirana I Zurich

www.ingramcontent.com/pod-product-compliance
Lightning Source LLC
Chambersburg PA
CBHW070934160426
43193CB00011B/1689